Surviving and Thriving in the Mad House of Youth Ministry

Keys to Longevity While Shaping Young Lives

Dave & Carole Nordstrom

WESTBOW
PRESS®
A DIVISION OF THOMAS NELSON
& ZONDERVAN

This book is a work of non-fiction. Unless otherwise noted, the author and the publisher make
no explicit guarantees as to the accuracy of the information contained in this book and in
some cases, names of people and places have been altered to protect their privacy.
WestBow Press books may be ordered through booksellers or by contacting:

WestBow Press
A Division of Thomas Nelson & Zondervan
1663 Liberty Drive
Bloomington, IN 47403
www.westbowpress.com
1 (866) 928-1240

Because of the dynamic nature of the Internet, any web addresses or links contained in
this book may have changed since publication and may no longer be valid. The views
expressed in this work are solely those of the author and do not necessarily reflect the views
of the publisher, and the publisher hereby disclaims any responsibility for them.

Any people depicted in stock imagery provided by Getty Images are models,
and such images are being used for illustrative purposes only.
Certain stock imagery © Getty Images.

Scripture taken from the New King James Version®. Copyright © 1982 by
Thomas Nelson. Used by permission. All rights reserved.

Scripture quotations marked (NIV) are taken from the Holy Bible, New International Version®,
NIV®. Copyright © 1973, 1978, 1984, 2011 by Biblica, Inc.™ Used by permission of Zondervan. All
rights reserved worldwide. www.zondervan.com The "NIV" and "New International Version" are
trademarks registered in the United States Patent and Trademark Office by Biblica, Inc.™

Scripture quotations marked (NLT) are taken from the Holy Bible, New Living Translation,
copyright ©1996, 2004, 2015 by Tyndale House Foundation. Used by permission of
Tyndale House Publishers, Inc., Carol Stream, Illinois 60188. All rights reserved.

ISBN: 978-1-9736-7472-6 (sc)
ISBN: 978-1-9736-7471-9 (e)

Library of Congress Control Number: 2019913973

Print information available on the last page.

WestBow Press rev. date: 09/13/2019

Contents

Pain – It is the single word that I could have used to describe myself as a teen. As the son of an alcoholic, my home life was a warzone. I was overweight and bullied relentlessly at school. Truly I felt unlovable: even by God!

When I first walked through the doors of Dave and Carole's ministry, I expected the same rejection I had experienced in the world. Instead I found a place of fun and laughter. A place of love and encouragement. An environment that allowed us to speak our minds and feelings openly about God, and yet firmly pointed us towards the truth that is Jesus Christ!

In the pages of this book you are going to find the formula that packed the room with teens week after week. The guidance on how to build solid personal relationships with teens, and the wisdom of over 35 years of youth ministry work. You are going to find the tools to do what was done for me, and thousands just like me: love and encourage we lost teens all the way to the foot of the Cross!

- Richard Wayne Holmes Jr.

Dedication

Carole and I are dedicating this book to the people who have been instrumental in helping us become who we are. These people have prayed for us, taught us through their actions, and loved us unconditionally.

In Memory of our granddaughter TaNyia, who left us to be with the Lord in (year) at the tender age of three and half years old. She was our ministry mascot and taught us tremendous lessons about life.

Paul and Ruth Nordstrom (Dave's Parents)

Gordon and Jean DeRidder (Carole's Parents)

Also dedicated to:

Don Windmiller and Peg Windmiller, Doug and Donna Fagerstrom (Dave's youth pastors & wives)

Larry and Elaine Gavette (Carole's youth pastor and wife)

Great Aunts Ella, Agnes, Besse, and Deena - Dave's Great Aunts who prayed for Dave as he grew up, and for Dave & Carole through their marriage and youth ministry.

A word of appreciation also for Craig Cramblet, a youth pastor who worked with us to start our outreach work with youth. His partnership was strategic in getting this ministry off the ground. As of this writing, Craig is Senior Pastor at Olivet Church in Muskegon, MI.

Thanks to John and Linda Carmen for adding their professionalism for the purpose of proofing this book

Credit also goes to our children, Angela, Taylor and Makenzie, who taught us priceless lessons in. Now that they are adults, I often wonder where they got their wisdom. Probably from their mother.

Acknowledgements

Those who contributed to this book

To give proper credit, I would have to acknowledge everyone in our lives. Everyone who has touched our lives and impacted our work with kids.

Youth work can be uplifting and satisfying, and it can also be downright defeating. For example, one day, Carole and I were especially discouraged after meeting with a group of teenagers for lunch time at school. As was my habit, before leaving the school I always went into the principal's office for a chat, and he would ask me how things went.

That particular day I confessed, "I don't even know why I try with these students sometimes. The stuff we talk about goes in one ear and out the other."

In response to my lament he said, "Every time you meet with students, no one leaves the room the same as they were when they came in. Every night you go to bed a different person than you were when you woke up that morning. Even if kids don't appear to learn from something you tell them, they *are* impacted in other important ways. They learn that someone cares for them enough to come to school every week, and spend time with them. They learn about being a part of something bigger than themselves. They learn respect, and manners, (like how to eat as civilized human beings). They watch you wait until everyone is seated before starting the meal, they observe how you and Carole treat each other as husband and wife, and the list goes on. They are watching you and taking it all in every minute you are with them, regardless the circumstances."

I never forgot that conversation, because it perfectly described the relationship Carole and I had with him and his wife, Cheryl. Richard Smith was the principal of that particular school and Cheryl worked there as a teacher. For decades they mentored us through their everyday living and their profession. Jesus flowed from them to anyone nearby.

I especially want to acknowledge the Board of Directors for Make a Difference

Ministries. We had been doing outreach to teenagers through our affiliation with Youth for Christ for 30 years. As we launched Make a Difference to continue our outreach to lost teenagers, they believed in us enough to jump in with both feet. They are all still hanging in there with us. What a gift! Thanks Richard and Cindy Lindrup, Richard and Cheryl Smith, Ric and Dee Scott, Dan and Lisa Morse, Jerry and Pauls Ellis and Heather Ruffin. You are all constantly a huge inspiration and support to Carole and me.

The lifeblood of the frontlines of any ministry are the leaders in the work. The leaders that dedicate their time to Make a Difference Ministry are second to none! Each of them is an inspiration to us. We have learned more from these dedicated people than we could have ever taught any one of them. All of the incredible people connected with this ministry are an inspiration to Carole and me.

They are the epitome of people that we respect. Some have been with this ministry for twenty to thirty years. Thanks to all of them for their great service to God and youth

Foreword by Tom Coverly

I will never forget a particular time I was traveling to speak at one of Dave's youth meetings. I saw a hitch hiker and though I'd never picked one up before, I decided that day to do so. He needed a ride for only a few miles. I told him I was about to speak to a bunch of teenagers. We quickly began talking about things of the Lord and before we both realized it, we were headed completely the opposite way that he needed to go. We both laughed about it; I turned around, dropped him off where he needed to be, and drove to the youth event.

I share this story with you, not only because of its connection to the Nordstrom's, but also because I believe we all need to focus on our direction. Let's be honest, a great amount of wisdom is needed when dealing with teenagers. If we don't receive direction, we can get distracted and find ourselves heading the wrong way while making poor choices.

I have been involved in youth ministry for twenty-four years as a former youth pastor, Christian music venue owner, and currently as a nationally touring youth speaker and comedy magician. I have spoken to nearly three million young people all over America. The more I speak, the more I discover I need to learn.

This is what I love about Dave and Carole's book. Right from the start, Dave admits how little he knew as a young youth worker. I can only dream of having the kind of knowledge and wisdom he's shared in this book at my fingertips when I was in my twenty's, a youth pastor right out of college. You will find this book is real and raw. Dave and Carole are true heroes of faith, like the book of Hebrews talks about. Their passion is real, and their hearts are genuine, as you will quickly see. I have witnessed their passion first hand at many youth events, and have seen the way the students love this powerhouse couple.

I encourage you to learn from their mistakes. Learn from the times they headed in the wrong direction. The insights in this book makes it a must read for every youth worker and will get them started well. We are in this journey together to make a kingdom impact in student's lives.

Many blessings as you go where God has called you to go.

Tom Coverly

What will You take from this Book?

This book is not filled with Bible verses and theological statements. It contains forty years of timeless youth ministry lessons, addressing issues and questions like:

- Is youth ministry really your calling?
- Insights for the spouse of a youth leader.
- Turning weaknesses into strengths.
- Motivating teens in your group.
- Make sure you are getting personal value from the right things.
- Effective ways to recruit and maintain volunteer leaders.
- Avoiding burnout.
- The importance of holding your ground on issues.
- Understanding the human nature of teenagers.
- The importance of knowing your own limits.
- How to know if or when you're too old for ministry.
- Staying true to ministry through culture change.
- Admitting "I don't know" can be a ministry opportunity.
- Connecting with that trouble maker student using an underrated ministry tool.
- Why little old ladies can break the stereotypical youth volunteer mold … and MORE!

My Official Apology to Parents

When I was a young youth worker without kids of my own, I knew much more than I know now, or so I thought. I was the "professional" youth worker. I knew teenagers. After all, I had been one. And I went to college for a special degree so I could become a "professional" in youth work.

Now that I am on the other side of raising my own children through the teenage years, I would like to make an official apology to all parents concerning every piece of advice I gave them about teenagers. I knew nothing! I am still learning, as we parent our adult kids, and help to raise and nurture our grandchildren, the oldest of whom is a teenager.

Introduction

One Couple's Youth Ministry Journey

My name is Dave Nordstrom and I have been working with teenagers since I was twenty years old (in 1975), beginning my career as a college intern at a church junior high ministry. After getting married in 1979, my wife Carole and I spent a few years in different types of youth work. We tried working with mentally challenged young people, as house parents in a juvenile detention home, and working as youth directors at a church. I finally ended up working with mainstream high school teenagers, most of whom had a skewed view of Jesus, if they knew anything about him at all. Eight years after graduating from college and getting married, I began my work with high schoolers in the Youth for Christ ministry called Campus Life. My youth work career spanned the changes from using a mimeograph copy machines in the 70's (ask your grandparents what that is) to all of the modern computer equipment and technology.

In my early days as a youth pastor, not making very much money, or having access to seminars and training, I wish I could have found a book that was a quick and easy read, and would have given me some insights as to what was coming. So as I am now into forty plus years of youth ministry, I will attempt to share the challenges and failings I experienced in those years. And I will pass on the lessons I learned and the growth that took place in my life and work, to those willing to learn from my mistakes.

Since my wife and I have been not only marriage partners, but also ministry partners since 1979, this information would really be incomplete without her insights and perspectives. We've worked together well at times, and at other times not so well. But we both have been committed to God, to each other, to our children, and to youth ministry. No matter what the situation, we've been committed to stay the course, yielding to our calling from God to work with teenagers, as long as we are able.

For what it's worth, here are some of our insights. I know that you'll make mistakes, just like we did. But at least this information can help you learn from our specific errors, and even take what you thought were weaknesses, and turn them into strengths.

Chapter 1

A Word of Caution to Freshly Married Couples

I will begin this section with a friendly warning. It may seem that I'm sticking my nose into your situation without even knowing you. I can remember people giving me this warning when I got married, as we began work in full-time youth ministry one week after the wedding. I was too impatient to get into ministry and their warnings fell on deaf ears. This caution may also fall on deaf ears with many readers. You may be impatient as I was and move forward into your ministry career too early. But I need to at least try to make the case that you should wait, and adjust to your new life as a married couple before plunging into ministry.

When you're young and full of energy, you are usually also excited about your future. And sometimes that excitement leads to a lack of patience, moving forward into a career that you may not be ready to handle.

My wife and I got married after my senior year of college. It had been Carole's freshman year. I was twenty-two and she was eighteen when we got married. We immediately got jobs two thousand miles from home. Our schedule, as my final year of college wrapped up, consisted of graduation, a couple of weeks later a wedding, two days later Carole's nineteenth birthday and two days after that moving way to begin our new life as youth workers at a church. No honeymoon and no time to rest or process anything. It was a whirlwind. We just wanted to get going with life.

The church put us in charge of the junior high rather than high school ministry because we were so young, especially Carole. We were excited and threw ourselves into the work. With so much going on at the church, and so many people asking us to get involved in other church activities, we didn't get much time for ourselves. As the work continued during our first year there, the lack of time we had to invest in our marriage wore on us. By the end of our first year, we had a pretty weak relationship.

Let me speak guy-to-guy to any man reading this. In case you don't already know, men and women think differently about family and career. We guys pretty much focus on one task at a time. When I was single, I focused my energy on getting a girlfriend and building on that relationship. When I met Carole and our relationship grew, I focused on trying to get her to marry me. Once we were married, I moved on to the goal of launching my career. As we began our careers as youth workers in our first church together, you guessed it! I was focused on being the best youth worker that I could be. My thinking was that having completed the marriage task, it was time to focus on a new task, my career. Meanwhile, my wife's focus as a newly married woman was to be the best wife she could be. Those two things proved to be in compatible. Problems began to creep in until we felt that we had to give something up in order to save something else. It was an ultimatum: our work at the church or our marriage. I've made some bad choices in my life, but fortunately through Carole's wisdom I was able to see that our marriage needed saving, not the career. Even though the ministry was booming, we were on the same page to protect our marriage.

If I had the opportunity to do it all over again, knowing what I know now, after our wedding I would have taken a year, or maybe even two, to focus on our relationship with God and each other. I've seen so many young couples make the same mistake that we did: getting into ministry too early in their marriage. Unfortunately, several of them ended in divorce. Though you may not be asking my advice, I'm going to give it anyway. If you value your relationship with God, your spouse, and your future career as a youth worker, give yourself some time and space, and please don't jump into youth related endeavors too soon. People who need what you have to offer will still be there when the time is right for you to begin. God has all of that under control.

A good way to start would be to have a "regular" job, with set time off to spend together. Volunteer with a mature youth group, learning from that vantage point. Your future self will thank you.

Carole's Note

Women, we were created by God to be helpers to our husbands (Genesis 2:18 NIV). We need to be just that, offering listening ears and= helping hands in ministry and marriage (Ecclesiastes 4:9–12 NIV). And we need to be willing to say something when we know there is a problem. When our husbands are overworked and being taken advantage of by their church, after much prayer we must lovingly point out issues we see. This includes specific times when the church has expected too much of him, or instances where he could have said no. Friends, our time to say these things is not after a youth group meeting or—worse—after a church board meeting, when our husbands are tired and just want to relax. The right time is after a period of rest, when they are ready to hear our concerns. Also, your best ally could be the pastor's wife. Ask advice. Seek wise counsel from board members. But do not talk about your husband behind his back, complaining about him. He needs your support and love, not another critic.

Your marriage and your family are worth protecting. Any church who expects your husband to be on call twenty-four/seven is not the church for you. Everyone, especially newly married couples, deserves days totally away from work and the demands of the ministry.

Chapter 2

Are You Sure You Really Want to Do This?

Ever since I was a teenager, I knew that I wanted to do what my youth pastor did: dedicate my life to working with teenagers. I thought, *"Wow! Hanging out with teens, playing basketball, and going on trips sounds like a perfect job."* It sounded fun, and I would never have to grow up. I was in love with the idea of going into a great line of work, but for all the wrong reasons. I think that happens a lot when you look at something from the outside, without understanding the realities.

After high school, I went to college to begin to prepare for my youth ministry career. My second senior year (I crammed four years into five), as I said before, I met the woman who would become my wife. After graduation, we got married and I took a job as a junior high youth pastor at a church in Denver, two thousand miles from where we grew up. I was twenty-two and ready to get away from my hometown and see the world. My wife was nineteen, and her one year at college was her first time away from home. See any potential problem yet?

The problem was that we weren't ready to get into this together. We needed time to acclimate to each other. We needed time for our relationship, marriage, and partnership in life to develop. Ministry is a lifestyle and can be very invasive. We needed to be locked together as a couple making the decision about going into this challenging work. It's a team effort and required both of us to be open and transparent in the ministry. Both must be ready and willing to go into it, locking arms and ready for battle.

Looking back, one thing that we were never good at was prayer time together. You can never pray too much (1 Thessalonians 5:17), beginning with praying about our own relationship with God, our spouse, kids, ministry, provisions, and so forth. One thing I failed at as the leader of the home was to develop prayer with my wife and our kids. My wife was the prayer warrior, which was a strength where I was weak, but that's another ministry truth that will be covered later.

You can never know for sure what you're getting into, and you can't be prepared for all that is going to happen. But being locked together with your spouse (if you have a spouse), bathing things in prayer, and developing your relationship until you believe that you are ready for something like this together is vital.

Carole's Note

Never quit praying for your husband (Philippians 4:6–7 NIV). He needs your prayers, and you know him and his needs better than any other human being—even his mother!

Also, nagging him to get him to pray with you doesn't work. I learned that the hard way. Much of the blame for our lack of prayer time as a couple falls on me. Rather than praying for God to work in his heart, I nagged and bugged and whined. Of course he wanted to run far from that!

God is much better at prodding our spouses to do what is right and good. Let him do his work.

Chapter 3

Youth Ministry Is a Calling from God

When the time is right for you to jump into ministry here is something to consider: I think that working with teenagers is sort of like liver. You will come across people who *love* liver and people who *hate* liver. And although they are probably out there, I have yet to talk with anyone who says about liver, "its okay, I guess."

Working with teenagers is the same way. People will either *love* working with and being around teenagers or they will *hate* it, especially when it comes to middle schoolers."pIt would be impossible to count how many youth workers I've talked with over the decades that got into youth ministry as a stepping-stone to something "bigger" .And as I think about it, there is nothing wrong with doing things that way. These folks seem to think of youth work as training for what they really want to do with their lives. During the time they are working with teenagers, not only are they learning and growing, but the students are also getting a good youth worker.

The person who gets into youth work to stay, and wants to make it a career, is much harder to find. God has given them a taste for working with teenagers that will last a lifetime. Speaking for myself I think career youth workers have an aversion to totally growing up in certain ways. We want to stay connected with young people because it energizes us. And I've heard it said that a good youth worker had ADHD as a kid and has lots of energy as an adult.

I felt the call into youth work when I was pretty young. I am the kind of person who wants to make a mark in the world, and a difference in people's lives. I thought it would be awesome if I could make an impact on teenagers' lives like my youth leader had in my life.

I went through high school and college and still wanted to work with teens. When I met the woman who would become my wife, and discovered she desired the same thing, I saw it as another piece of the puzzle God was using to move me and us in that direction.

After we failed miserably at our first youth ministry position, we spent about two years trying different jobs. We were miserable in every one we tried. I took the experience as confirmation that I was still wired and called to be a youth worker. I just needed time to mature and grow.

When we felt we were ready we tried it again. We experimented with different kinds of youth work as I mentioned before. But when we finally joined Youth for Christ (YFC), reaching lost teens, something clicked and I knew that was where my passion finally found a home.

Because my wife and I worked so well as a team we dove into it together.

Carole's Note:

Ladies, if you are married to a youth leader you *are* in ministry. The ministry needs you as much as it needs him. The teens need your presence. If you have another career and children it can get hard to be involved. But find a way to be there, even if it's one night a week for two hours. The teens benefit greatly from seeing the two of you together as a married couple. The girls want to know you and need you to feed into their lives. You are also getting a front row seat into your husband's life. You get to see what makes him tick.

Another reason to be involved is protection. Your presence puts a wall between your man and teenage girls in a youth group. You might think it could never happen to your husband, but given the right circumstances, many men have been tempted and given in to the temptation to be inappropriately involved with a youth. Your husband is human and teen girls can present a temptation. Your presence reminds him and the teens that he is a married man. It can also protect him from outsider's suspicions and possible accusations of inappropriate behavior between your husband and the teens, even when he's innocent.

Again, you are his number one prayer warrior. You need to see his work first hand to know how to pray. What better way to do that than to be present?

Chapter 4

God wants our Obedience more than our Talents

Early in our years of ministry I worked full time with Youth for Christ (also referred to in this book as YFC). The moment we stepped into this ministry, working mainly with unchurched teens, we felt that we had found our niche. We had tried a number of different types of youth work but we instantly fell in love with this ministry. We were highly motivated by the potential of this work and were determined to be successful at it. Teens were coming out to ministry events and many were coming to Christ.

But it's important for you to know that as employees of YFC we were responsible to raise our own financial support, covering salary and benefits. Finances were a constant struggle. We were new to the area in which we worked and it was going to take some time to gain trust from people, businesses, and churches with the potential of supporting us financially. We experienced times when there just wasn't enough support coming in for us to get paid. We had traveled thousands of miles away from everything we knew in order to be part of this ministry and we wanted to continue. So Carole took on a part time job at a Christian bookstore and I did some odd jobs to help make ends meet when financial support for the ministry was inconsistent and low. However, going twelve and sometimes sixteen weeks without pay was just too overwhelming financially.

At the peak of one of those times I drove my car to the Youth for Christ office thirty minutes from our apartment. I was desperately hoping and praying that the mail would bring in enough financial support to at least get something towards our sixteen weeks of back pay. I arrived at the office praying that when I walked in the secretary would say, "It's a miracle!" as her desk was overflowing with support checks. But when I walked in the opposite was true. Absolutely no money had come in that day.

I worked in my office for a while and headed back home. I had five dollars in my wallet. That's all the money we had. We had nothing in savings, nothing in checking. No cash laying around the house. *Nothing!*

I stopped at a gas station to put the last of my money in the gas tank. A man came up to me and asked me if I could give him money for something to eat. I thought about that last five dollars and the gas I badly needed. Whenever someone asks me for financial assistance I have a test for them. I say, "I won't give you money but I will buy you something to eat." If they continue to press for the cash I figure they're not telling the truth and want to use the money for something else. If they are telling the truth they will take me up on my offer.

This time the guy said, "That would be great" and I thought, "Oh shoot, there's goes my last five bucks." I took him to a nearby fast food place and bought him some food, hoping maybe I would get some conversation out of the deal. But as soon as I handed him the bag he tore into it, walked away, and the food was gone in a minute and a half.

I walked back to my car, and was about to pull out of the parking lot when I remembered that I had left something at the office. I drove back there and as I walked through the door I witnessed an unforgettable scene. On the secretary's desk was a mountain of envelopes, all piled in the middle. The secretary was standing next to the desk with her hands over her mouth in disbelief. I asked her where all the envelopes came from and she said a bag of mail had gotten misplaced at the post office. The mailman made a special trip to deliver it. Over the next few hours we went through the mail. There was enough money in those envelopes to catch up on our back pay, plus some more.

What I learned from that experience is this: it's hard for us to give up control of ourselves to God. If there are two ways to deal with a situation, to do it ourselves or to rely on God's provision, we are tempted to do it ourselves. Then we can say, "I did it." As long as I had that last five dollars in my pocket I had some resources of my own. Once I gave that money away I didn't know if I even had enough gas to get home. When I gave up my very last dollar the control shifted to God. I had no resources left to my name. My thought at the time had been, "My wife and I have given our lives, along with our gifts and talents, to God. So why is he letting us go through this?" The answer came to me that God wants our obedience more than the gifts and talents we bring to the table. As long as I had that last five dollars I had resources, and I believe God wanted me to rely totally on Him

That lesson came up a number of times throughout our ministry. As humans we're proud to be able to say, "I did it myself." The Bible is replete with stories of God letting his people get into situations so dire and hopeless that the people couldn't possibly say "I did it." This is one of those lessons that will be with us throughout our lives. We don't seem to ever learn it completely. When we get into hard situations, after trying yet again to "do it ourselves," God reminds us that it's about obedience to him, not about how gifted and talented we think we are.

Carole's Note

Money is one of the top stressors in a marriage. Take that stress down to a manageable level by letting God guide you. Trust him; he has promised to provide. Also, remember that God put the husband as the head of the home, as stated in Ephesians 5:23(NIV). "For the husband is the head of the wife as Christ is the head of the church, his body, of which he is the Savior." Be willing to help the situation in any way possible. For me, it was getting a job and being very frugal in all our spending.

As you talk about finances and giving remember that God gives us the ability to speak our minds, but don't put blame or pressure on your spouse. You could push him to move to work where he is paid more, more consistently. But think of all the blessings you would miss out on by doing that!

Chapter 5

On what do you Base your Personal Value?

I believe defining personal value is generally very different for men than for women. When Carole and I got married we moved to Denver, Colorado to start our first youth work together. It was a middle school ministry. I was twenty-two years old and Carole was nineteen. We had only been married for about a week – our honeymoon consisted of driving out to Denver to start the job. As of this writing we've now been married forty years and have never really taken a proper honeymoon.

Later in our marriage we studied the differences between men and women (beyond the obvious) and realized that what we did as we started at the new job illustrates the classic difference between men and women. Carole had decided that she was going to be the best wife she could be. That was her personal goal once we got married.

Men tend to achieve one goal, and then set out on the next one. So my goal of getting married was reached and my mind was set on the next goal, which was to become the best youth worker that I could be. My and Carole's goals conflicted. Once we were married her journey to her goal began – to become a great wife. Our marriage resolved my goal of getting married and I was on to the goal of developing my career.

Where was God in all this? What Carole realized some time later is that she was focused on pleasing me instead of pleasing God. What I realized later is that I wasn't focused on pleasing God at all. I just wanted to become known as a great youth worker. That was my goal.

So the advice we want to pass to you from our failure in this important area is to aspire to what God wants you to be. Your youth ministry is an overflow of who you are. If your motivation is wrong, your ministry will be off course. So draw close to God first

(Mat. 22:37). Love and honor Him. And desire to be the unique person that God wants you to be. The result will be God forming you into the person that is best for your spouse, your marriage, and then your ministry (Matt. 6:33). If you look to your spouse first at some point you will be let down. When you look to God first you will never be let down.

Carole's Note

If you put your relationship with God first you will become the best wife you can be. Another hard lesson I learned during those first months of marriage is this: don't expect your husband to provide your happiness or your self-worth. You are asking too much from him. You are in control of your life and your choices. Be a unique person apart from your husband. This will enrich your marriage in so many ways. It gives you value and a brighter outlook on life in the process. A resulting perk is becoming more attractive and interesting to the man you love!

Chapter Six

Setting Limits

As I've shared when Carole and I were first married and doing youth ministry, our initial task together was running a junior high ministry for a church. It didn't have much money to give us so the church offered a very nice parsonage for us to live in. And even though our salary was only eighty dollars per week, we never saw a house or rent payment, or a utility or repair bill. That was huge for us in our first year of marriage.

So, the beautiful thing was that we got to live in the church parsonage and receive the financial benefits that went with it. But on the other side of the coin, the thing that burned us out the most was that we lived in the church parsonage and all that went with it. What I mean is we were right next door to the church so we were never really off duty. People would come over needing this and that at all hours of the day and night. And when someone would come over and we would explain that we need some time away from church responsibilities they would come back at us with, "It's just one thing. Can't you help us with just one thing?" What they didn't realize was that dozens of others were coming over for help with "just one thing." And it added up to no time off for us.

Earlier, while visiting that church to be considered for the job, my former youth pastor was also working in the area and Carole and I went to visit him and his wife. We thought we'd surprise them and just drop by their house. I wasn't sure exactly where their house was so I called them from a gas station nearby. He answered and I told them that we wanted to visit them. He replied that it wasn't a good time – I would have to visit another time. Wow! I thought I had just been snubbed. Here I was two thousand miles from home, wanting to visit my old youth pastor and friend, and he turned me away. I couldn't believe my ears. I thought he would be excited to see us. I just didn't understand.

Fast forward to almost one year later. We had been on the job for about eight months and I now understood what he was talking about. He was setting limits. He and his wife probably needed some time together and away from ministry. But hey, we were just one couple who wanted to visit just one time, couldn't he accommodate us?

Later, that was exactly what happened to us and we were burning out fast. We needed some time away. The pastor tried to help us by letting us use his trailer at a camp ground in the mountains and we took him up on it. But then we were back home and back to the grind. We were too young and insecure to turn people away and say no when we needed to. We actually ended up doing things like parking our car down the road, and keeping all of the shades closed and lights out when we needed a break. That worked somewhat, but it was too little too late. We already felt so burned out that all we wanted to do was to leave ministry and move back home.

As we've grown up, become more secure in ourselves, and gained more experience in ministry we've learned to set limits and say no when we need to. You can feel when the burn out is coming (See section on "watching your gauges" in Chapter 33, a concept from Pastor Bill Hybels). Your body will tell you when it's beginning to feel exhausted; your psyche will tell you when it can take no more, etc. Listen to your body and watch your gauges to know when it's time to back off or risk being burned out. Carole and I put a system in place where we take time away from ministry and even our own kids. When you allow every emergency to become your emergency you will be overwhelmed. Multiply that by however many people want your help and you can see the potential problem.

I don't know your individual situation, and I realize that you have ministry responsibilities that must be accomplished for your job, and your paycheck. But with that in mind, do what it takes to set limits and watch the gauges that tell you when it's too much; set those limits and say no to people. You will ruffle feathers and people's feelings will get hurt (even family). But do what you must do to protect yourself, your marriage, and your time especially if you intend to stay in ministry long term

Carole's Note

The ideal time to set limits is before being hired. You and your husband should discuss the issue before you go to an interview. What are you willing to do and when? If the church or organization can't give you time off to recharge it's not the ministry site for you.

Chapter 7

Bigger and Better are Not the Same Thing

I grew up attending a huge, wildly creative, and very spiritually effective youth ministry at a local church. Later, as I got into youth work, I found myself using that experience as a template for my own ministry. My goal was to have a huge youth group. I thought that big was the same as successful. During the first several years of our ministry I struggled to grow a large group. I would get so frustrated because I couldn't seem to draw lots of teenagers, and so I felt like I wasn't being effective. I was running YFC Campus Life groups in homes at the time and would get anywhere from two to twelve students at a meeting. I remember the feeling of failure I had one time when I planned a big event at a school. It was called a Burger-Bash (an old YFC event). The cost to get into the event was one dollar and kids could eat all the burgers they could stomach. I was planning for at least a hundred students and got twelve. The event was right across the street from the school. I felt like a total failure. I'd tried to make the event as teen friendly as I could and twelve was all the students we could draw.

As a Campus Life Director I had the whole community to draw from, as opposed to a church youth program involving only students from families who attend the church. Yet numerically I still had the smallest ministry in town. I was constantly comparing myself to other youth pastors and was always jealous of the things they accomplished. But I kept going, trying to be as effective as I could in the kids' lives although our numbers were small.

Years later I ran into former students who began their walk with Jesus during those years when my youth ministry programming drew small numbers. As I interacted with more and more former students I found that not only were most of them still living the

Christian life, but many had gotten involved in ministry where they were currently living. I then began to realize that big isn't always the same as better. Sometimes better does come in small packages. I am not implying that you shouldn't strive to reach out to as many teens as possible. There are some leaders who are very effective with large numbers. They know how to draw students and use the staff around them in amazing ways.

But there is only one you.

There is no one on the planet with your particular genetics, gifts, talents, traits, and desires. In your uniqueness, God may have created you to be able to reach and connect with that one teen and lead them to a relationship with Christ.

I know this is hard for a young man (or even an older man for that matter) to hear because of our pride and our ego, and maybe even our competitiveness. But if your group is small and you are working your hardest I hope you don't do what I did at times, which was to forfeit the quality of pouring into the kid's lives because I was so focused on wanting to have a large group. (For more depth on this subject refer to chapter 32).

Who knows, you may be pouring into one teen and he or she may impact many more than you know about.

An example is a young man I worked with through Youth for Christ. I recently learned that his time with me in that ministry "changed his life" (his words). What he went on to share in his message to me would about knock me out of my chair as I read it. He said that he never imagined that making a decision to follow Jesus as a fourteen year old boy in a small Campus Life meeting would have resulted in his becoming a chaplain in the army impacting thousands of U.S. Soldiers and possibly civilians in Iraq.

Here is another example. Carole ran a teen parents ministry for about twenty years. She poured a lot of time and energy into one young pregnant teen girl. When you invest in someone you can't know what the result will be. Will this teen make something of themselves or will they be a waste of time, humanly speaking? This girl was determined to make it. She eventually married a great guy and had two more children. She also went on to college and nursing school. There had been times when she seemed to need more than we had to give but Carole stayed with her. She is now a head trauma nurse in a hospital, a staff member in our youth ministry, and serves on the board of directors of the new youth outreach organization we started.

We are not saying that someone has to be successful in order for us to feel they warranted our time. But we wonder what impact Carole's time had on her life. Where would she be if someone hadn't believed in her and spurred her on to push forward? My point is that when one of your students becomes a person of influence and goes on to impact many lives your small ministry is multiplied. It only takes one.

So although I know first-hand how hard it is on a guy's ego to lead a youth group with just a few kids in it, you never know what potential those kids may have and how God will use them. They deserve the same amount of effort and commitment as a group of kids in a large ministry. Never underestimate the impact you have on your students whether you run a tiny ministry or a large one.

Carole's Note

As a woman seek out a student each year to spend extra time with and pray that God places a special young lady in your life that you can impact for him. The rewards you will receive are amazing!

Chapter 8

We is more Effective than Me

Everyone internalizes things differently, probably based on their life experience, the way they were brought up, and their personality. I was raised up in the mid-fifty's to the early seventy's and our family was big on the idea of taking personal responsibility for your own behavior. As a result I had a hard time with the team concept. Being the leader in a youth organization I believed everything that happened, success or failure, was on my shoulders. I know that ultimately the responsibility of the program is on me, but what I'm talking about here is the day to day running of the ministry. I would forget I had a team of people with me who were willing and able to take part of the load. When we had a success we all celebrated it together. But when there was a failure, I felt I needed to carry the burden of the failure alone.

On one occasion, after an event had flopped big time, we were sitting together in a staff meeting and I was very apologetic to the staff because I felt as the leader the full responsibility of the failure was on my shoulders. One of the staff spoke up and told me that we were together in this ministry, as a team. If an event failed (from our point of view) we failed as a team, and if it went well we succeeded as a team. The other staff agreed. Their words and attitude really encouraged me and gave me a whole new outlook on events. I was so relieved to hear them verbalize their support of me and their sense of ownership of our work. They let me know loud and clear that even though I was willing to take the brunt of the blame they weren't willing to let me do it. Though the event seemed to be a flop it was a milestone for our team as we bore responsibility together.

And I realized another truth. When something doesn't go as planned the weight of the disappointment and the feeling of failure is so much lighter if you have a team approach and each person takes a part in the responsibility. Together you can encourage each other as you try to figure out what went wrong, gang up on the problem, and deal with it as a team. Because *we* is a much better approach to ministry than *me*.

Carole's Note

When your guy comes home after a tough meeting it's time to let him have his time to vent and try to build him up. He needs to know that you still think he's worth something. Remind him of other times when things went well, and maybe even remind him of times when things seemed to go poorly but God used it in spite of the problems.

Also, there is so much value in giving your husband time to go out with his volunteers or a trusted buddy, to just let off steam and be a guy and not the one in charge. Encourage Christian friendships and try hard to let him go now and then. It doesn't mean he loves you less or doesn't want to spend time with you. It means that he's a well-rounded individual!

Chapter 9

Setting the Tone for your ministry, Right off the Bat

In our ministry we work with many at-risk teenagers. Actually, mostly at-risk teenagers. I believe all families have dysfunction. It's just a matter of degrees. I also assume that most churches and youth groups are having to deal with an increasing number of severely dysfunctional families. Of course the result is dysfunctional, messy teenagers. Most of the church youth ministries that I am familiar with draw the same percentage of at-risk teenagers that we do and our mission is to seek out those kinds of kids.

Having said all of that I'd like to share a classic story of how, if not properly dealt with, a dysfunctional teen can affect an entire youth ministry. A fifteen year old girl who came to our teen program brought with her a different drama every week. At first it seemed pretty harmless, and not many kids paid attention to it so we just let it go. As the weeks went by the drama became more and more intense.

Like the old theory referred to as the law of diminishing returns, you don't get better results from repeating the same behavior. So you accelerate things. As a simple example, a person doing drugs has to do more each time in order to get the desired effect. You can't go back to a lesser amount and expect to feel the same high.

This particular girl progressed her drama to the point where it began to negatively impact the group. In one instance during a meeting she skipped out with a boy and spent youth group time down by a nearby lake. Her mom came to pick her up after the meeting and she and the boy came around the corner of the building. She ran up to my wife and hugged her good-bye. Then she skipped up to her mom's car, waved to everyone, and left.

Late that night, her mom called us. She reported that the boy had attempted to rape her daughter. She was calling from the hospital where a doctor was examining the girl for signs of physical force. This crisis went on and on, eventually to the point when Carole and I were contacted by an attorney and subpoenaed to testify in court. The stress of it all was really intense.

After that experience we made a decision as a staff to set a tone right from the start of the year, squelching drama wherever we saw it begin. We give a speech at the beginning of each year about behavior, what we tolerated and what we didn't. Usually that wasn't enough. We had to be prepared to enforce our boundaries somehow, which could mean kicking a teen out of the group. Teens needed to know we were serious about backing up our rules.

We try to minimize distracting outside influences from coming into our meetings and have procedures for doing so. Usually a drama occurs when someone brings a personal problem into the meeting from the outside, attempting to get the other kids tied into it. When that happens we connect the student with a staff who will try to help them work through the issue. Often a student will resist the staff's help because they're less interested in solving the problem than in the attention they receive from others as a result of it. If they are not interested in having a staff help them and continue to create drama in the meetings they are asked to leave, not just the meeting and the building, but the property as well.

We've learned from experience that if the disruptive student stays on the property other teens will see them standing outside in the parking lot looking forlorn and want to go out and try to help them. Also, if they are still on the property the drama king or queen, no longer able to use their issue to get attention, can turn to other disruptive behavior like breaking into cars and draw the attention of the police. To prevent that potential we always have people at our events and meetings who cover security. They make sure the person leaves the premises and stays off. We can then can continue our event, ministering to kids who want solutions for their life not just attention and drama.

Since we've been taking the approach of laying out the rules and setting the tone for the ministry at the beginning of each year, and dealing with the rule breakers before they escalate, ninety-nine percent of problems created by a drama king or queen were eliminated. The kids who really are having personal problems and want to deal with them are free to find real solutions. The other kids don't have to worry about them and can participate in the event. Of course, occasionally we need to remind the kids what the expectations are for their behavior and what the result will be if that expectation is not met.

Carole's Note

This type of situation is another reason why being involved in your husband's ministry can be so important and helpful. When you spot a teen starting to draw attention away from where it should be you can be a barrier. Being the wife of the youth leader gives you some clout. Use it. Go to a teen, ask to speak with them, and try to disarm the drama that is unfolding.

Equally important is that you and the volunteer team are the best defense against a lawsuit based on "their word against yours." It's an ugly truth that you need to be constantly aware of. A teen or a parent could accuse you or your husband of a wrong action. With a good volunteer team and an effective and consistent strategy to "nip the problem in the bud," these kinds of accusations are less likely to result and you will have good evidence of innocence if needed.

Chapter Ten

When a Student is removed for Behavior Issues, I Always Give Them a Way Back In

One of our female students was involved with something that caused dismissal from the group meeting. This particular incident was actually the "last straw" involving behavior that was very disruptive and destructive to the group, and to herself. Since there was a major rainstorm going on that particular night I didn't want her to wait for her ride outside. So, after having her call home for a pickup she stood inside near the door to wait for her ride to show.

Without warning she flew into a rage. From the back of the room she started yelling and swearing at me. She called me horrible names while I was up front trying to lead the meeting. I asked one of the female staff to take her into another room to wait. That wasn't effective and her behavior and language were really upsetting the rest of the students. I asked the security person to take her outside so she could wait for her ride in the rain. In a few minutes they showed up to take her home and I realized the driver was actually another former student who had also been kicked out. I called her home to let her mom know that she had left with another student.

I had a feeling, from previous experiences, that she would try to show up again the following week and get on our bus at one of the bus stops. I gave instructions to the driver that no matter what this girl was *not* to get on the bus for any reason. Sure enough, when the bus arrived at the youth group the bus driver said that she had shown up. He didn't let her ride but he handed me a note she had given him for me.

The note was full of apologies. She said the youth group meant so much to her that she didn't know what she was going to do without us. She asked what she would have to do in order to make amends and rejoin us. After some time in thought and prayer, along with advice from other staff, we came up with a proposition for her. Because she had trash talked the youth program so much, we told her that if she went the rest of the school year without saying anything negative about us we would consider allowing her to rejoin the following year.

The incident occurred in March so she would have to wait until the following September. When September came she contacted us and seemed to have behaved herself. We decided to let her come back for a probationary period of time. She then asked about C.O.R.E.(Connect, Overcome, Restore, Endure-They are taught the importance of CONNECTING with God. God will help them OVERCOME the baggage they carry around and even into the relationship with God. God will RESTORE them in many ways and help them ENDURE in their relationship with Him and living a life in love with Jesus in front of their family and friends). Core Group is are also are involved on the inside of the youth ministry, helping plan and put together events and meetings. They are also deeply discipled by the staff. She had been a part of this group before and wanted back in.

We told her that if her good behavior continued we would talk about it for the following year. She eventually made it back to Core Group and graduated out of the youth program in good standing.

When a student does something to cause us to expel them, resulting in them losing status in some way, I like to make it possible for them to change their behavior or attitude and be able to make a come-back should they choose to do so. Some students want that and some don't. The way back is provided and it's up to them whether to go for it or not.

In this case the student lost all of her position, honor, and status in the group and it was a one year process to gain it back again. She was willing to put forth the effort to make her own return possible.

I think of how Jesus deals with us when we struggle or fail him. An example is how he dealt with the disciple Peter, who denied knowing him at a crucial time (Mark 14:66-72). We all mess up and make bad choices, and Jesus always makes a way back for us. By doing that Jesus modelled how we can treat people who fail us in some way. We have found this approach to be very effective when handling disciplinary issues in our group.

Carole's Note

All I have to add is to be a good listener. When your husband has a situation like the one Dave shared, listen to him as he works it out. This isn't the time to badmouth the teen or the parents, but to pray for wisdom and guidance for how to best reach a reasonable disciplinary action.

Chapter 11

The Solomon Years

I remember when I was a teenager, brought up in a Christian home, very involved with church, and having parents and an extended family who I could look to as models of the Christian life. We grew up with good, solid morals and I felt that I had a pretty defined conscience. So, how could it be that for a couple of years after high school I seemed to drop off the deep end morally, even while attending a Bible college?

As I reflect back wondering what prompted that behavior, I think it was a combination of suspecting that I was missing something and being curious about it. I wanted to figure out if the faith in Christ my family taught me was mine or if I just went along with it because my family believed it.

As I work with students I notice that generally they go through the same process after high school. What I've observed in teenagers is that during the ages thirteen to seventeen they are used to having their lives run by someone else: parents, teachers, other relatives, pastors, and other authority figures. In fact, any adult usually has the say over you when you are a teen. As a teenager reaches eighteen they become legal adults. However, they are still used to having their life run for them. As their eighteenth year of life moves forward they hear both adults and other teenagers say, "you're eighteen now, you're an adult." So as they hear that more and more we can see the change happen. They start believing they are adults and the "you can't tell me what to do" mentality begins to take over.

By the time students are nineteen that thinking is in full swing. Looking back I realize that was the time when most of the problems between my parents and me took place. And as a side bar, I think that this tension is necessary (I would even call it a gift from God) in order for us to break away from our parents, and begin the process of becoming independent and eventually ready to start our own family. If kids remained at the maturity level of ages ten or twelve parents would never want them to leave, which is not really healthy. They need to move on and the growing tension between them and their parents is a major factor that sparks it.

As young adults reach the age of eighteen through the early to mid-twenties (sometimes this can take longer than just a few years) I have asked them why they sometimes act out in ways they know to be wrong. Many have told me the same thing. They say something like, "If I'm going to believe the stuff that I was taught as a kid I need to compare it to other ways of living to see if it's really truth." They usually don't say it in a profound manner, but that's basically what they're saying.

Even with all of the Bible training, time spent with them, and all of the good things poured into their lives a parent should not feel like a failure or that they are losing their children during this challenging time. It is the natural process that kids go through after they leave the nest. They test limits, they experience life, and they might even go to a dark place in their lives for a while. They may not know why. Often young people find it necessary to test the truths that parents and others put into their lives. I believe one of the applications of the verse "Start children off on the way they should go, and even when they are old they will not turn from it" (Prov. 22:6, NIV) is an assurance that if we put the truth in them, in the right way, they will have that truth to compare to the darkness around them in the worst of times. I've learned that when someone compares darkness to light, most people will choose to come back to the light of the truth.

The key here is to make sure they have the truth taught to them in a way that relates to their lives, connects with their experiences, and makes sense to them. Not only must it be heart-felt, but make sense intellectually as well. Keep on keeping on in a young person's life and don't get too discouraged when they go to the dark side for a while. Most students are just trying to figure life out for themselves.

The one thing that you can do during that time in their lives is pray for them. I usually pray for the youth we work with in the same way I prayed for our own children, who have gone through their own dark times. I ask God to keep them safe as they seek the truth. My prayer is that God will keep them from permanent harm or damage as they search out and test the truths on which they will base their life. I am certain that the only reason I am where I am today can be credited to the fervent prayer of some saints in my family.

Teach them the truth, model it, and pray for them. That's our responsibility. The rest of the gain is God's. "I planted, Apollos watered, but God has been making it grow." (1 Cor. 3:6 NIV)

Carole's Note

God is the only one who can see the future. He is the only one who can watch over someone at all times. He is your link to that teen or young adult that has gone astray. Stay close to God who is keeping watch on the wayward person. When hope seems lost picture yourself walking with that person towards the throne of God. Talk with God, giving him your sorrow and frustration. Then visualize yourself releasing the hand of the searching, lost person to God's hand and walk away. God never expected you to carry that load alone. Freed of the burden, you can focus on what is in front of you, and minister to others.

Chapter Twelve

God Prepares and Calls us into a Certain Work Based on how He wired us.

As I stated before, when I was ending my high school years and moving on to college I had the idea that I wanted to be a youth worker but really had no clue what that meant. And if the youth work thing didn't pan out I at least knew that I wanted to work with people in some capacity. I'd always been a social person and loved working and spending time with people.

God had my course already charted out for me. And I was in for a big surprise. When I graduated college, with the help of one of my former youth pastors, I was able to land a job working with junior high students in a church. I thought, "Here we go!" This is what I had gone to college for. I had dreamed of doing this kind of work and here I was at the threshold of my future. I was finally a youth pastor in a church.

Here's the ironic part. Off and on during high school I attended the Youth for Christ ministry called Campus Life. I remember the Youth for Christ director waiting outside our high school to meet students. He wasn't allowed inside the school, so he patiently waited outside and as I passed him he would say hi to me. At one point I turned to my friend and said, "Now that's a job I would *never* do… be a Campus Life Director."

Fast forward: I was at my dream job, working as a church youth director. But the longer I worked in that role, the more I realized that the work wasn't as satisfying as I dreamed it would be. I went through youth work experiences that I thought would be "it" but none of them were right. All the while, one ministry opportunity kept coming up and I kept pushing it back down. It was Youth for Christ.

Whenever I thought of Youth for Christ I kept remembering the Campus Life Director at my school, who was doing a job I knew I would hate doing. For three years I struggled with different positions as I avoided anything to do with Youth for Christ because I was *sure* that was *not* for me. Reflecting back on that time I was like Jonah running from what God wanted him to do. And as with Jonah (Jonah 1-2), I felt that God put me in a position where I had to face and accept His unique calling for me. Youth for Christ came up again. This time I stopped, listened, and heard what God was saying to me, "Just trust me on this one." It was like a mom with a spoonful of food trying to convince her little child. "Try it, you'll like it!" With my back against the wall and being out of options, I'm embarrassed to admit my reluctance as I finally took the step and trusted God.

That was 1984, and my wife and I spent the next thirty years working with lost teens thru Youth for Christ, and we loved it. God had wired me for an outreach ministry to teenagers that other organizations have given up as lost. I have no desire to do anything else with my life as far as a career goes. I've found where I fit. It's a great feeling and I totally have God to thank for it. If it was up to me I would have missed it.

God designed each of us for a specific work. Let Him help you figure it out. After all, God is the one who created you and wired you the way you are. I used to think that when we deal with God it's a clash of wills. If God's will wins, then mine loses. And if my will wins, God loses. But I found out that if God's will wins everybody wins.

Carole's Note

If you allow God to change your heart your desire will be to serve Him. Pray often throughout your life for God to lead and guide, and give you a love for the ministry He has blessed you and your husband with. It's a joy to have both you and your spouse going in the same direction – the direction God has for you!

Chapter 13

God gives us the Love and Passion for what He calls us to do

After I graduated from college and got married I began my first job working with youth. For the next four years I journeyed through four different positions, trying to figure out why none of them seemed to click with me. I just didn't have peace and joy working in any of the roles I had tried up to that point. But there was one opportunity that kept pursuing me. My youth leader during middle school kept contacting me, asking me to work with Youth for Christ. I kept telling him that I wasn't interested and went on with my own journey, checking out youth jobs that just didn't seem to click with me or my style of ministry.

Finally, frustrated with it all, I took a job at a local lumber yard. Now if I thought I wasn't happy in some of the youth jobs I had up to that point, I had no idea how much I was going to hate working in a lumber yard during a Michigan winter.

Then my former youth leader called me on a day when all I wanted to do was to get as far away from the lumber yard as possible. I told him that I would accept the job. Within a couple of weeks we moved from Michigan to North Carolina and began our work with Youth for Christ. Almost immediately I fell in love with the mission, the work, and the kids we were dealing with. It seemed Youth for Christ ministry lined up perfectly with the gifts, talents, and desires that God had given to me.

So a light went on in my life. This is it! This is what I'd been searching for. These kids reminded me of myself growing up. They needed love, acceptance, and affirmation that they were loved for who they are. They were lost in many of the same ways that I had been lost. That was 1984. As I write this book in 2019 my wife and I continue to work with the same kind of teenager.

God called me, before I even knew it, to work with lost teenagers in Youth for Christ. And He gave me a love and passion for the work. All I had to do is follow Him to the venue where He wanted me to use the love, passion, and gifts He'd blessed me with.

So I guess the point of this section is to not be afraid to try things. God may have you working in the most unlikely places with the most unlikely people. Maybe it's something you never thought you'd be happy doing. Yet you find yourself happier, more content, and more effective than you ever thought you would be. God knows what he made you for.

Along with the gifts and skills that God has been developing in you through various life situations, He will also give you a love and passion for the work He calls you to do. This also may surprise you. You may find yourself loving something in a way that you never thought you could.

Carole's Note

Your husband finds much of his self-worth in his career. It might take him a few moves and changes before he finds the right fit. Don't be discouraged with this phase. Remember that God is your constant. God can bless you both in your relationship with Him and with your husband through these times. And these trial and error times make for great stories later in life!

Chapter 14

Finding your Niche

There will be people who go in and out of your life advising you about what you're good at, and what you're not good at. They will tell you what you should be doing with your life. And you may even find some of their ideas attractive and think you'd like to try them. But stay focused on God's call. Believe me, if you divert from it, you might be excited about it for a while. But eventually, when the excitement wears off, and you're not where you're supposed to be, you will be miserable.

On the other hand, when you are in your niche, exactly where you know God wants you to be, situations may come about that make you feel miserable but at the same you will still have the "… peace of God that transcends all understanding …" (Philippians 4:7 NIV).

When God worked it out for me to go into Youth for Christ, I resisted, because I didn't think it was what I wanted. I thought, "Here it goes, this is what I feared when I became a Christian. God would call me to some place, to do something that I will be miserable doing." For me, that was Youth for Christ – remember the YFC Director that was standing outside my school and I decided that I would never want to be that guy?

When it comes to a battle of the wills, if one loses the other wins. But I found out that when I listened to God and went into a specific ministry within the general calling of working with youth, if God's will wins I win too. If my will wins I lose.

When I listened to God, even though Youth for Christ was the last ministry on earth I thought I would be happy with, not only did God give me the desire of my heart, (Psalms 37:4) working with youth, he also gave me a specific ministry where I could live out my calling. The ministry I thought I would hate I love. And there is no other type of ministry in which I'd work.

And let me tell you. When you listen to God's calling and are in the niche in which you are supposed to be there is not a feeling that compares. When it all comes together, you will know you were born for this specific purpose.

Carole's Note

I read Genesis 3:16 in the New Living Translation and a light went on. I finally understood why we had so many marital problems. As God doled out the discipline for disobedience in the garden he said, "You will desire to control your husband, but he will rule over you." But my goal is to live the way God intended – as a helper to our husbands, making an impact on those lives around us, whether they be teens, parents, or my own family. You will experience the blessing of a strengthened marriage if you follow God's plan.

Chapter 15

You may lose Happiness at times, but you never lose your Joy

As I was talking about God's calling on your life I referred to happiness and joy. Through nearly forty years of youth ministry we've been in situations that have caused us unhappiness, and I can remember going to bed sometimes with knots in my stomach or headaches. Working with people will do that. And I don't doubt that I have caused some knots and headaches for someone else.

About fifteen years thru my youth ministry career I learned something very important. I used to think that the verse that tells us to consider it pure joy when we face trials of many kinds (James 1:2 NIV) "was crazy. Not just joy. Pure Joy! What?

I questioned how I can have joy when things are miserable? After I'd been in ministry for a while, someone explained to me the meanings of the two words happiness and joy. Then the verse made a whole bunch of sense. The word happiness is connected with "happenings." So the emotion of happiness is based on something happening to me. If the situation is good then I'm happy. And if things are difficult I'm not happy. Being happy depends on the situation. Whereas joy has a different context. Joy results from having our state of mind focused on the knowledge that there is someone bigger and more powerful than ourselves, the heavenly Father who loves us more that we could possibly love ourselves. He always has our best interest at heart. So, whether things are happening that are good or bad we can have joy. And joy is what will get us through the tough ministry times, helping us to stay focused on what God has called us to do and to "Press on toward the goal to win the prize ..." (Philippians 3:14 NIV).

Carole's Note

Choose to see joy. Focus on positive things in your husband, in the ministry, in your life. Where your heart is focused will change your outlook on life and on the work you are doing.

Chapter 16

What Geeks You?

There are a lot of tools out there that will test your personality and gifts to see where you fit into ministry and those are great to take advantage of if you can. When we first got into ministry we received advertisements sent to us and to the church offering a personality/ministry test. The problem was, we only made eighty dollars per week at the time and couldn't afford to pay the money it took to use those tests. Now there may be some tests like that on-line that are inexpensive or even free.

You may need to take the personality test, but I know of a free way to discover what ministry suits you. I call it the "What Geeks Ya?" test. It's pretty simple and self-explanatory. And other people may see the answer in you before you identify it for yourself. If you're talking about going into ministry but aren't sure what you're best suited for ask yourself this question, "What about ministry am I excited to talk about?"

What makes your ears perk up when you hear someone else talking about it? What about ministry makes you want to walk across the room and join in on the conversation? What kind of ministry makes you become more expressive and makes your eyes light up when you talk about it?

When my wife and I are with groups of people, and we're all conversing, many topics will come up. But when the topic of youth ministry comes to the forefront Carole says that I come alive. My eyes get wide, I join in the conversation more energetically, and my voice gets louder. I generally become more animated as I talk and as I listen. And the whole time I'm listening I'm chomping at the bit to jump back in and talk. Youth work! That's my passion. And had I known then what I just shared with you I could have avoided taking expensive tests and spending a lot of time trying to figure out what type of ministry I was born to do. It was evidenced in my feelings, expressions, and excitement, and I never picked up on it.

Carole's Note

Help your husband figure out what kind of ministry is best for him. You see a side of him he doesn't see. And you are part of the equation. God would never expect the two of you to split over ministry. God ordained marriage as a sacred bond for life. As the two of you think, talk, pray, and try things together it may become obvious to one of you before the other. Pray together daily and then enjoy seeing the future unfold before you!

Chapter 17

Staying Focused on your specific calling is Crucial for Success & Longevity

Because I had been so impacted by a couple of my youth pastors I made a decision about my career path even before graduating from high school. I determined that youth work was going to be my career. I had no idea what that meant, or what it would look like, but that's the career path I set my sights on.

As I went to college periodically I would have some questions and doubts about my career choice. But I always came back to my original focus, which was becoming a youth pastor. Fortunately the woman I met my senior year of college, who would become my wife, had a dream of being a youth pastor's wife! See how the calling fits together?

But as I graduated and started life out there in the work world I found that there were many kinds of youth work. So which was I most suited for? I began to narrow it down by trying different types of positions that were available to me. First I tried being a church youth pastor. When you watch someone who is good at being a youth pastor they make it look very easy. The average student involved in a youth group doesn't see or experience all of the peripheral things that go along with being a youth pastor and I discovered it wasn't for me.

The next ministry I tried was working with mentally challenged teens and adults. And though some of the residents were adults, they general had the mental capacity of teenagers or even younger. So I felt like I was still working with teenagers across the board. But I was soon disillusioned. Most work with mentally challenged people I found available was in government run institutions. I wasn't happy working for a government agency because I felt that other things came before the betterment of the people they were supposed to be serving.

So I moved into another type of youth work. This work was a combination of private sector and government. It was correctional facilities for troubled teenagers. The kids in the facility had broken the law. First my wife and I worked for a private agency that was more of a house parent setting. We were responsible for twelve boys and were in a pseudo parental role. It wasn't a lock-up facility and the boys could run away if they wanted to. But when they were caught their next placement would a lock-up institution.

We were there for a year and decided that wasn't our cup of tea for the long term either. However, through that experience we learned things that would become foundational in our future work with students. Next we moved to work with teenagers in a lock-up facility that was also a combination of government/private institution. In two months I realized this work was absolutely not for me. But again, I gained skills that helped me in my future work with teens.

Then it happened! God moved me into a job that I had been avoiding for years, mainly due to the responsibility of having to raise our own financial support. I was sure I could not do that. But God kept bringing Youth for Christ up in my life and I kept avoiding it, convinced I was misunderstanding God's call.

As soon as I began working with Youth for Christ I discovered that the job I was dreading was what I was born to do. We struggled and muddled through with our fundraising efforts and kept going one year at a time. It's been thirty five years now. Thirty of those years were with YFC, and five with "M.A.D. (Make A Difference) Ministries, an organization we established ourselves.

Once you find your focus, stick with it. There will be many people in your life who will tell you that you are good at this or that. They'll tell you how much God could use you here or there. They might even go as far as to tell you that God told them that you are supposed to be doing the ministry they are describing.

My wife and I have dabbled with trying to start a junior high thing, a college thing, or a big brother type thing. But as soon as we began to go off into other directions it started to dilute our focus, which was working with lost high school students. When people give advice as to what God might want us to do it's always tainted with personal bias. One time when I was struggling with making a decision a youth worker colleague who had much to gain by me making a particular choice told me to listen to counsel, but not to let counsel drown out what God is telling me.

So as you have people surrounding you while you are in youth ministry telling you what they think you should be doing, or adding to your work, stay focused on what you know is God's call for you and your spouse. I think continued focus on your specific calling from God is one of the secrets to longevity in ministry.

Carole's Note

The world has different goals and rewards than God offers you. His rewards are better than anything humans can offer! Don't think "promotion" is always a good thing. It might be, but it also could be a door to total frustration and loss. Enjoy the work God has called you to do.

Chapter 18

Ministry will be greatly Enhanced when you have Teenagers of your Own

When I was a young youth worker I saw myself as a "professional," qualified to give advice to parents (when they asked) about their teenager. After all, I had been to school, got a degree, and it really wasn't that long ago since I had been a teenager myself. I was very anxious and excited when a parent would ask me how they should deal with their teenager. I had all kinds of advice and was glad to give it out.

Now, as I look back after raising three teenagers I am embarrassed and yes, even ashamed, about most of the advice that I gave to parents. I realize now that I had no clue what I was talking about. A degree in youth work is no comparison to the humility and wisdom that comes with raising your own children and teens.

So, my advice to you as a young youth worker is this. You do have a different perspective to share. You have some youth work education, some life experience, some gifts and talents. But please remember that raising your own children gives you a perspective that you cannot get in the classroom, or with any other kind of life experience. (And no, having a dog or cat does not count as being a parent, no matter how much you see your pet as a part of your family). There is no relationship that compares to the parent-child relationship. No matter how much time you spend with teens it is absolutely not the same. I believe that a parent/child relationship is the only relationship that can happen without strings attached. Your children are your children and no matter what they will always be your children. I think God gives us a fierce love for them that lasts our entire life. It's a very unique relationship that you cannot duplicate in any way. You need to go through it to understand it.

Remember your own position in life as you give advice to parents. In fact, there was a time a parent called me about problems he was having with his son. He said that his son didn't have any interest in church. Because I have three daughters and no sons I shared with him that I really couldn't relate to his problem. Instead, I connected him with a guy that I have much respect for and is a great dad for two sons. That was probably the best advice I could have given him.

Connect a concerned parent with someone who has proven track record in their area of need. If you don't feel you have the life experience that relates to issues with their teen it's alright to give insights you may have for him or her. But don't be afraid to say, "I'm not sure if I can help you with that problem but I think I know who can."

Carole's Note

Women have a different way of communicating. As females we have insights and perspectives our husbands don't have. A good rule of thumb is this: if a mom comes to talk about their teen, I talk to her. If a dad comes to talk about their teen, Dave talks to him. We have also met with couples together.

Chapter 19

Go with your Gut and Own your Feelings

I don't know what your background is but as I was growing up my self-esteem wasn't very good. I carried that issue into adulthood. I assumed everybody was better, smarter, and faster. If I was confronted by someone about something I assumed they were probably right and I was likely wrong. I didn't speak up for myself, but rather just kept quiet even when I thought I was I had a valid point to make. As I got into ministry as a twenty year old I still had a problem speaking up for myself and for the teens that I was working with. It was easy for people to manipulate me spiritually.

Here's an example. I was in the hospital in my later twenty's with bladder cancer. Some people from a church visitation ministry came to my room to visit me. They told me that I had cancer because somewhere in my life I was disobedient to God. That comment devastated me. I fell for it hook, line, and sinker. I carried that load for a long time. Then it dawned on me! "If being disobedient is the rule for getting cancer, why doesn't everyone have cancer? After all, we are all disobedient at one time or another." But it took some struggle and time before I came to that sensible realization.

After being in ministry for a while and growing spiritually, as well as learning things about human nature and having an encouraging wife, I began to gain some self-confidence. I began to handle things differently. At one of our Youth for Christ meetings a local church showed up and said they wanted to pray for us. I thought that meant they would mix in with the crowd and silently pray throughout the night. But what they did was to make a big scene, gathering together, dramatically praying. It was disruptive and made the students, who were mostly unchurched, very uncomfortable.

I approached them and asked if they would stop the big scene they were making because it was scaring the teenagers a bit. They replied that I was quenching the Holy Spirit and that they needed to pray in that manner. So I asked them to leave.

As a result they made a real scene, yelling at me and letting me know that I would pay for this decision eternally for not letting them do their thing, their way. I was persistent and they finally left. I knew that they would start spreading criticism around the community about us (which they did). It was a risk I was willing to take. I had experienced this type of disruption before, and by letting it go on I lost a ministry to a whole school. The students spread word around their school to stay away from our program. Because I'd developed more confidence in my experience tested wisdom I was able to take a strong stand and not let it happen again.

I share that painful story to say this: "own your feelings." Another way of saying it is go with your gut. What I mean is that if you are feeling a certain way in a circumstance you can be certain that others in the group are feeling the same way. I was very uncomfortable with these people doing what they were doing, and I'm a Christian. I could only imagine how the students who weren't Christians were feeling.

In certain situations you may sense something one way but then think, "I'm probably the only one feeling that way." I can tell you that you are not! I'm not saying that you should overreact. I'm just saying that you are probably feeling what many or maybe even most of the people in the room are feeling. So as the leader be confident and react the way you think you should, knowing how it might affect kids and the ministry.

I use the "go with your gut" concept as part of our leadership training, especially for small group leaders. In small groups there are usually one or two students who seem to want to monopolize the time thinking everyone in the room is interested in their life more than any other. But others in the group need a chance to be able to talk. If as staff you have concerns about how the small group is being affected the rest of the group is probably feeling that way too. The leader needs to make sure that the time is balanced with all students being able to speak if they wish. Let the student who is monopolizing the meeting time know that what they're saying is valuable, but that there is a limited amount of time and others need to have a chance to share. Offer some time outside the group to speak with them. They may or may not accept that invitation depending on the reason for over sharing. Was it just to gain attention from the group? Or is there a real need that needs to be heard with appropriate help offered?

This concept can also apply to other situations in your youth group. Just remember, what you're feeling, others are likely feeling as well.

Carole's Note

Dave said it all!

Chapter 20

Vacations can Suck the Life out of you or Save you!

Early in my youth ministry career I never wanted to miss anything. That's the only reason I can think of to explain what I am about to tell you.

When I would go on vacation the secretary would take calls for me, very efficiently take a message, and tell the person that I would return their call when I got back from my vacation. When I would return from vacation all refreshed and ready to go I would go to the office and she would hand me a three inch thick stack of messages needing my response. Just seeing a stack that thick made me feel overwhelmed. It would take me two weeks to unwind and in the first few minutes back at the office I was already feeling stressed.

An older and wiser youth pastor who had gone thru the same thing gave me this advice. "Give your secretary these instructions. Ask her to tell anyone who calls for you that you will be returning on a specific date. If they still need to contact you they could call back then." What a HUGE difference that made. I found that most of the people who contacted me never called back. They found an answer to their dilemma another way.

Another way to use vacation wisely is to leave town. We have spent many vacations at our home because we live on a lake. Why spend the money and go to another lake? The problem with that is that people can still find you! Ministry, being a different kind of animal than other types of work, will continue to try to draw you into a situation even though you're on a much needed vacation. Either put your car in the garage, lock your doors, and keep your lights off or leave town. Go where no one can find you.

If you do a vacation right it can save you from burning out. If not it can suck the life out of you.

Carole's Note

I see it like this: you want to relax or have some fun without being the youth leader. Do all you can to help make it happen. Don't bring up work on vacation. Agree on a vacation where you both can unplug and unwind. Connect with each other and your children. Vacation is not a time to visit a ministry supporter. It's not a time to take in a conference on the joys of youth ministry. It is a time to recharge.

Chapter 21

Learn from Everything you do, and Use it

When I first decided to get into youth work I tried working in different venues to see which one best suited us. Among them was working at a juvenile detention campus. It was not a lock-up facility. That was the next step for these boys if they ran away from this facility or if they were too much to handle in this venue. This was their last chance before going to juvenile jail.

This particular facility was on a large piece of land with four homes surrounding a huge pond. Up the hill from the homes were other buildings: an office, apartments for staff, a garage for working on vehicles, etc. It was out in farm country so if a boy ran away he had to travel quite a way on foot in order to reach a neighboring home. It also was a beautiful spot and gave the boys some experiences they might not have had where they came from like horseback riding, farming, swimming, and hiking to name a few.

Carole and I first went through a training time and then were fill-in staff to give the fulltime house parents of each of the four homes time off each week. We went into the facility figuring that these boys didn't have good relationships with older men in their lives so I thought I was going to be their pal. As we entered one of the homes we were taken under the wing of a much older couple who were grandparents. Their life experience dwarfed ours. Everyone called the house father Uncle Lee. As he watched me interact with the boys he immediately pulled me aside and said, "What do you think you're doing?" I didn't really understand the question so I asked, "What do you mean?" He saw that I was making the biggest mistake most people make coming into that situation. I came in to be a pal rather than an adult and an authority figure that was there to guide and model life as an adult man in a family situation. That's what the philosophy was – to set up a home with a married couple and six to nine boys who would interact like a family. Uncle Lee saw that I was setting myself up to be walked all over by these boys. The first piece of advice that he gave me was something I would use in every ministry that I would be a part of from that time forward. He told me "You always want to start out your relationship with these boys with a sterner manner. Later you can always lighten things up bit. But if you start out light it's much harder, and sometimes impossible, to become stern."

What great advice and seemingly so simple. But obviously it was a concept I didn't understand when I first got there. I used that counsel in every ministry that I was involved with as I worked with teenagers. It was also great advice for me as a parent. We're not the teenager's pals, we're the adult figure. That's not to say that we are hard core or mean. We can be very relational and at the same time hold on to the authority status that we need in working with teenagers. Teens have plenty of other pals in the form of their peers. I see a lot of youth workers who are in their forties wearing teen style clothes, getting the same tattoos as teens, talking like them, etc. I don't believe that youth, especially in today's society, need an adult imitation of themselves. They need an adult model they can look to in the next stage of their life. I think it's ideal for young people to have a positive role model they can refer to in the next stage of life. An appropriate example gives them the specific qualities they can aspire to as they get older.

In the end that venue of residential youth work was not for Carole and me on a long term basis. But I learned so much from that would be applicable to my ministry of reaching lost teens in the mainstream of society. And I not only learned from other youth positions but also from all of my various roles, secular or Christian, youth oriented or not. Life experiences are like gold and are applicable to any job you choose as your life career.

Carole's Note

As we journey through life God adds the blessings of multiple experiences. Some are frustrating, like being a house parent when we are not cut out to be one. Keep a positive outlook, encouraging your husband and yourself to look at it this way; you learn, move on, and keep looking for your passion. When you find it, you know. And all the experiences from life will make it that much sweeter! No paycheck or prestige is worth being in the wrong career. Keep moving forward.

Chapter 22

You cannot duplicate the Moving of God's Spirit

I mentioned in another section how I have been burned by allowing myself to be spiritually bullied by people with an agenda. As I have grown and matured, accumulating more life experience, I've learned to stand up to people when that happens. But on the down side it has put me on the defensive when approached by people sharing spiritual things with me. It's brought me to the point where I am currently, which is that if I'm going to make a mistake spiritually I'm going to make it on the conservative side. What I mean is that when I am faced with something that I think has the potential of turning the kids off or damaging them spiritually I shut it down. I have a big problem with people who manipulate the emotions of teenagers.

But what I fail to realize sometimes is that most teenagers live life through their emotions. That's why I believe some of them go forward to accept Christ at meeting after meeting after meeting. They need that emotional reassurance. So they are very emotional beings, and though I try hard not to use or manipulate that aspect it's good to realize that emotions are also something God can use to turn a kid's life around. Staying close to the vine (John 15:1-8), to the mind of God (Romans 15:5-6), and the working of the Holy Spirit (1 Thess. 1:4-5) is key as you minister to teens.

Here is an example of what happens to me - maybe you can relate. If not you're probably more mature spiritually than me. I'm in a large group meeting with our students sharing a story and giving them a challenge about something to do with God and them. As the challenge progresses I have a sense that it would be a good opportunity to give an invitation for them to respond to the gospel. It could mean asking them to come forward, or raise their hand, or suggesting they follow a staff member out of the room to meet with them.

Then I remember some of the ways I've seen kids' emotions manipulated. For example, once I offered an invitation at a meeting and a student came forward and just lost it, crying his eyes out. He then stopped coming to the meetings and avoided me at school. I found out later it was because he was embarrassed to have broken down in front of everyone and felt he was manipulated.

When that thought hit me I buried the idea of doing an invitation. But after the meeting things happened that made me realize the Holy Spirit had been prodding me to let God get involved in the meeting. So what is my response? I felt bad that I didn't respond to the Holy Spirit's movement like I should have. The next meeting I tried to re-create the movement of the Holy Spirit. And of course that didn't work. I lost the opportunity and the only thing that I could do about it was to try not to miss the next one. It's not an easy thing. Our feelings combined with our past life experience can deceive us. So our means of knowing how to respond in a situation is by staying deeply connected to the Jesus the vine, the mind of God, and the working of the Holy Spirit.

Carole's Note

Many times couples are made up of one person who is more emotional and one who is more analytical. It is a God-given blessing. We are a team. We can hand the baton to the other when needed. When Dave gives the challenge to the youth I can watch the crowd, lingering on the faces of those I can see are emotionally connecting to what is being said. I can pray for the kids as they listen. I can pull one aside and offer to talk further with them after the challenge is over. There are a number of ways you can be a supportive member of the team. Each personality offers something. Each volunteer or staff member can be used by God to cover the bases, even if another member of the team seems to drop the ball. Keep your eyes wide open for you opportunity to connect with students during those times.

Chapter 23

Your Spouse and you have Different Strengths. Use them.

Carole and I had very similar backgrounds in areas like family upbringing, church, and life experiences. We both felt a calling to do ministry – specifically youth ministry. As we got into ministry we always participated and led together. We were partners in ministry and seemed to balance each other out because despite similar backgrounds we had different talents, interests, gifts and personalities. When we were younger some of those things would irritate us about each other and would seem to be the cause of tension between us. But as we grew and matured we figured out that our differences, the qualities that made us argue sometimes, were the exact same things that, when used in the right ways, made our ministry together better. We began to study books on gifts and personality differences. We figured out what talents each of us had. We became more purposeful in using those gifts to the advantage of ministry. If you want a great resource for developing that type of teamwork in ministry go "old school" and find Gary Smalley's *Keys to Successful Relationships* and his personality quiz. It not only changed our marriage, it changed our approach to our work with lost teens.

Here's a very basic example of how we work together. When we studied the personalities of men we found that they are headline or umbrella oriented. What that means is men focus on the big things. When we would go on a picnic I might pack the hot dogs, drinks, watermelon, and things like that. My wife would take care of stuff like napkins, silverware, and condiments.

I remember going on an outing with a few staff and students. We were taking my boat to a lake to do some water skiing and tubing. My wife couldn't go so I packed all of the stuff for the picnic and guess what happened? That's right! We had all of the food, drinks and even a watermelon but no cups, plates, or plastic silverware. Nothing to cut the watermelon so we just broke it up and ate it with our hands.

Now when we do events or even our weekly meetings I organize the event and take care of the headline responsibilities while Carole fills in all the details. When people ask me questions about what Carole was in charge of I used to try to answer them (actually I still try sometimes). But now I just refer them to Carole because I mess things up when I try to do Carole's job. I just stick to what I do: plan and put together the event. If I didn't plan the event there would be no event to work details up for, and if the event is planned and the details aren't what they need to be the event is a flop.

That is one very basic example of how we work together using our gifts and carrying out our individual responsibilities. We complement each other in ministry. As I am finishing up this section someone called me and asked me about some details of a fundraising dinner that we are putting on for the ministry. Finally, after nearly forty years of marriage and ministry together, I did the correct thing right off the bat and referred this person to my wife. Who says I can't learn? It just took a few decades.

Carole's Note

Make sure you listen to your husband. Spend time finding out what the event or the topic of the meeting will be. Read his notes or listen to him practice his challenge or sermon. You can't fill in the details without fully knowing what the headline story is to begin with. Never assume you know what he is led to share that week. Ask and listen. The details will then work well with the headline.

Chapter 24

There is a Time to let Students Go

The ministry I've chosen to be involved with in my youth worker career is reaching non-churched high school age students. When I first began youth ministry Carole and I were involved with junior high teens. The question that always haunted me was, "When do I let students go?" When I was a junior high director it was easy because I let them go to the high school director. When we started running high school ministry it became harder and more complicated.

The reason I felt haunted is because I was always afraid to let students move on in life if I felt I hadn't done absolutely everything in my power to reach the kids for Christ. If I could just keep them around a little longer maybe they would finally see the wisdom of beginning a relationship with God.

At first we allowed the high school students continue with the youth group until they were nineteen or even twenty years old. I refer to them as students because they were either held back in high school or were in the beginning of college. I know you might be reading this with red flags going up all over in your mind. But for me, as a younger youth worker, it seemed to make sense. I wanted to give these kids every chance possible to accept Christ into their lives before letting them go.

We did experience problems that always seemed to involve the older students somehow. I would find out at some point that problems were instigated, or kept alive, through the students that were really too old to be involved in the youth group anyway.

Then one year it all blew up. We found out that some of the nineteen and twenty year old kids in the group were having a very bad influence on the younger teens outside of the youth group settings. It got so problematic that I finally had to cut the older students loose in order to protect the younger, more impressionable ones. That caused the fire storm of the century. It was then that I realized the hold that the older kids had on the younger ones. The younger students looked up to the older ones and mimicked their behaviors. When I kicked out the older students many of the younger ones told me that if I didn't allow their return they too would leave the group and not come back. We stuck to our guns and as the year went on we began to lose students from the student leadership group that the nineteen and twenty year olds had their emotional hooks in.

We had started that year with twenty-five students that we called Student Leaders. Midway through the year we were down to eight. The effects of this would last an entire cycle of high school (grades nine through twelve). It took until all of the students that were around during that time graduated before we could really get past the impact of that event.

As a result we decided to make it a policy that the summer a student was eighteen years old would be when they should be graduating from high school if they stayed on schedule. Once they hit that point, whether they graduated or not, they needed to move on and out of the youth group. Since we implemented that decision we eliminated the problems connected with the older students. The ministry totally turned from constantly putting out fires to being able to invest in a positive way in the younger students' lives. It also made being involved in this youth ministry a whole lot more appealing and enjoyable.

A by-product of not allowing the students to hang on to the youth group when they should have left is that we saw them move on in productive ways. By allowing them to hang onto the youth group we were really doing a disservice. We were allowing them to be at a standstill in life instead of supporting their move on to the next phase. I explain that to them when they come to me and ask why they have to leave the group. Life is about progressing and moving forward. As much as I would love to have them around it's to their benefit to be encouraged on in their life.

To avoid the feeling that they were being kicked out we have a graduation ceremony from the youth program. We make them a graduation t-shirt, give them some spiritual growth teen reading material, and a box of candy. We have everyone else in the group say good-bye, doing it with flash and flare, making it all about them on their last night there. It turned out to be very effective and positive. They felt graduated out instead of kicked out. We assured them that just because they couldn't be involved with the youth program didn't mean we weren't still there for them if they needed us.

As I mentioned in the beginning of this section I didn't want to let them go until I had done everything I could to draw them into a relationship with God. I finally got it through my thick skull that it wasn't up to me to work in their hearts and turn them to God. It was up to God. That made it a lot easier to let them go. I couldn't change their hearts towards God. All I was responsible to do was to be obedient to God and do my part sharing Christ with them. The rest is up to Him. And it benefited everyone involved to move them on when the time came.

Carole's Note

That time was difficult. It was extremely hard on Dave. It was not a time for me to second guess his decision. It benefitted the whole group for me to stand with him, supporting the decision he made. I fielded phone calls from parents. I talked with teens who were hurt and angry. I prayed for my husband and the group.

I didn't want to let go of the teens any more than he did. But over time it proved to be wise to move them forward. It strengthened my faith in Dave's ability to watch the process unfold.

Our husbands need an advocate. They need to talk things out, working through problems and solutions. It's good for them to have godly, stable, and preferably older men to talk with. We (spouses) might be too close to a situation. Our feelings for our husbands can get in the way of doing the right thing. I wanted to lash out at the teens causing so much pain in Dave's life. I wanted to fix it for him. I wanted to quit and move on with our lives. But God held us up and guided us through the deep waters of the toughest time in our ministry.

Don't rely on emotions. Don't think you have all the answers. And don't give up.

Chapter 25

How we Treat Students can affect their Family for Generations

Twice a year, we take students on a retreat. Because most of our students are unchurched we introduce them to church attendance as we end our retreat by going to a local church service. Each retreat we try a different church to give the students an idea of what different churches are like. We usually pick one of the churches that a volunteer leaders attends.

On one occasion two boys were sitting in front of me during the church service. One of the student's families was part of a church so I knew he had a church background. The other student did not attend church, ever. About half way through the service the unchurched student's hand shot up into the air. The other student quickly grabbed his arm and pulled his hand down and said, "What are you doing?" The unchurched student said, "I have a question." The other student responded, "You can't ask questions in church!"

Unchurched kids don't know the Christian routine and react the way they do other at places like school, home, or with friends. It can be difficult navigating through a group of students who are partly churched and partly unchurched. And as we work through that situation we can make a decision that will affect a family for generations.

To illustrate, a while back I was talking with a youth pastor friend of mine who is part of a church that has a fair number of kids who come to his program who come from families that have nothing to do with church or any other Christian group. The teenagers whose families attend church basically know what's expected of them as far as behavior. For unchurched teenagers it's uncharted territory, as in the example I gave at the beginning of this chapter. The youth pastor shared that during their last youth group meeting one of the teen girls did something resulting in one of his leaders telling her that she wasn't welcome back to the church for youth group.

When my friend shared this story I thought of another friend of mine whose father was a pastor. She told me her father was treated so badly at the congregation that it turned her off to church and Christianity. To this day, as a married woman with adult children, she still feels the same way.

Now I will admit I don't know the details of what happened to cause my friend's student to be asked to leave the group but I share this story to make a point. I asked my friend if he knew the girl very well, or if she was a visitor, or a fringe student. He said that she comes from time to time so I asked him if he knew how to get in touch with her. My advice to him was to do all he could to connect with her and with the help of a female staff try to work something out for her to be able to make her way back into the group.

As I explained in an earlier chapter I believe in giving a student a way back to the group if they've been dismissed for poor behavior. It's their choice whether to accept it.

But here is my main point. This young teen could end up hating church and God, just like my friend did, and it doesn't stop there. The infection could spread to her children and even her grandchildren. Her entire extended family might hate church and God because of their family member's experience as a teen.

My youth pastor friend had a window of opportunity to change that picture by seeking out this girl and explaining some things to her, possibly creating an opportunity for her to come back. It would be beneficial for everyone involved in the situation, with the help of the staff who kicked her out so as not to disrespect the staff during the process, and provide a learning experience.

Because we've been in youth ministry for forty plus years we've seen generational things happen, both good and bad. I was glad to later hear from my youth pastor friend that he made contact with the girl and worked things out. It was good for her, good for the church, and good for future generations.

Carole's Note

When things go awry with a student or volunteer step in when it's appropriate, but you might not always be needed. We can make things worse by putting our two cents worth in where we shouldn't. Time can be a healer. Sometimes we can step up and be willing to help heal a broken relationship. Think of the above examples and how they could have turned out differently if someone had stepped forward and reached out to those involved and tried to mediate. But remember to keep emotion out of this one. A level head would be needed when others' emotions are running hot.

Chapter 26

Stand your Ground on Theological issues

As I shared earlier I was pretty insecure all through my growing up years. If I tried out for the school basketball team and there were twelve of us trying out I was sure there were eleven guys on the court better than me.

I could easily let myself get psyched out. As an eighteen year old high school student I visited a local college. The superstar of the basketball team came up to me in the gym where I was shooting baskets and asked if I wanted to play the game of one on one, up to ten. At that point I had no idea about his basketball skills. Over an hour later, with a huge crowd around us, he barely beat me. The score reached into the fifties and the game stayed close for quite a while. When I learned later who he was I could never come close to him in future match ups. My insecurities took over.

My personal insecurity affected me in many ways. I felt other's opinions and thoughts offered more wisdom than mine. I assumed he or she was more theologically knowledgeable and accurate than me. I was weakened in most areas because of my insecurities. I knew my Bible but was afraid that I might say something wrong theologically so I just kept my thoughts to myself and didn't challenge people when I should have.

Many years ago at a Campus Life meeting in a student's home a few adults came to visit from a local church. Things were going alright until one of them began speaking in tongues in the middle of the meeting. Then he took a couple more adults off to the side and started praying out loud, which disrupted the flow of what was happening in the meeting. I could tell the kids were very nervous and when I would say something the people speaking in tongues would turn and say, "You're quenching the Spirit." Well, I certainly didn't want to do that. We muddled through the meeting, with me sweating bullets. That night and into the next few days I got calls from parents firing questions at me about what was going on at the meeting. Some even accused us of being some sort of a cult. Many let me know that their kids would not be coming back to Campus Life ever again. I learned a lot from that experience. Though I believed I knew how tongues was supposed to be used (I Corinthians 14) I needed to develop some backbone in standing up to bullies.

The next time it happened I interrupted the meeting. I told the guests that their expressions of speaking in tongues at our meeting did not comply with the scriptural guidelines. When they responded that I was quenching the spirit I told them that I would be accountable to God if that were true. I knew their behavior was outside of scriptural bounds and asked them to either stop or leave.

I could see the teens were relieved. Most had never been to church and were not believers. They felt safe as they watched the ordeal unfold. I stopped a spiritual practice that was not following Biblical guidelines for its use. Although I would be considered a charlatan by some, I was never again going to be spiritually bullied or allow the students to be affected by it either.

Carol's Note

As Christians and as leaders we can be used by God in a variety of ways. Sometimes our gifts can make others uncomfortable. Our volunteers also have a variety of spiritual gifts. Try directing a volunteer with certain gifts to an area that fits your ministry. Hearing someone speaking in tongues can be scary for teens who have no knowledge of the Bible, for example. Figure out what gifts are best used and highlighted in different settings, and encourage those with different gifts to shine appropriately. Encourage teens to seek out a volunteer to take them to different church services, or to explain what the spiritual gifts are for and how they are used for God's glory.

Chapter 27

The Buck stops with YOU

Some years ago we went through a challenging time in the ministry, which I alluded to in earlier chapters of this book. I want to share more details about the incident in this chapter.

We'd had the practice of involving college age students as leaders in our youth program. This particular crisis came, however, when we discovered that some of them were involved in inappropriate relationships with the students. It all came to light during a retreat at a hotel. We assigned one staff member as security person to hang out in the hall during the night to assuring the students stayed in their rooms after lights-out.

The hotel was laid out in such a way that the security staff couldn't see all the rooms at once, so he had to make rounds. He came to my room in the middle of the night and let me know that a couple of the college aged guys had teen girls in their room. As a result the leaders and students were sent home immediately (after we contacted their parents).

The following week we had a staff meeting to decide what we should do with the college age leaders. Many of them had caused problems leading up to this incident, but we knew that this behavior was over the top and must be dealt with in a decisive manner. At the meeting some of the volunteer leaders shared the opinion that it was my fault we were at that point with the college leaders. I let them talk and as they continued the angrier some of them became.

I took it upon myself to accept responsibility for what they were saying. I am the leader and am responsible for the things that go on in the ministry. I was okay with accepting that responsibility.

But as this discussion got more and more negative one leader spoke up and asked,

"Why is this all Dave's responsibility? I thought we were a team. We were all around during this whole thing and should all take responsibility together for it."

That comment changed the tone of the meeting. The other leaders had a light go off in their minds, agreed that the ministry group was a team, and we needed to work together to lead it.

The bottom line is that as leader of a ministry the buck needs to stop with you, and becoming defensive won't help the situation. But laying all of the blame on the leader isn't usually fair. Your teams needs to know you can take the heat of the responsibility for problems and it allows them to feel they can do the same. Fortunately, in this situation, when one of the leaders spoke the others acknowledged he was right, and our meeting could become more constructive.

It's been said that leadership can be lonely at the top. That is absolutely true. But the buck needs to stop somewhere. And if you accept that, and acknowledge your failures, the surprising result may be that your leadership team will become stronger by your acceptance of weakness.

Carole's Note

As a spouse, you help set the tone. Many times volunteers will come to talk to you about your husband or about problems in the ministry. I think some people feel safer speaking to the leader's wife instead of the leader. How you respond can either add a lot of stress and anger to a situation, or it can diffuse it. Do your best to diffuse the issue. Your husband needs an ally. You know your husband's heart better than anyone.

Another point to repeat again is that you should give your husband down time after a meeting. When he walks through the door after a long night let him rest and unwind. Unless it is an emergency situation it can wait until morning.

Chapter 28

Don't Trick the Teenagers (The old Bait and Switch)

One thing I've always disliked is manipulation. So I'm conscious about not being manipulative with others. I think if God wanted us all to follow Him He could have easily created us to robotically be a follower. But He chose to create us with a choice, which for obvious reasons can be a curse or a blessing. God could also appear to the world and end, once and for all, the debate as to whether He exists. God has reasons for why He is doing things the way He is doing them. I believe it has a lot to do with our choice. God wants us to choose Him without His manipulating our choice.

Have you ever been invited to an event and attended it, only to find out that it was nothing like what you were told it would be? Don't you hate it when that happens? I've accepted those kinds of invitations and I felt so ripped off and manipulated.

In the Christian outreach world that kind of tactic is pretty much accepted and even expected. We promote something as fun, exciting, and full of energy. When the students get there we throw in some fun so as not to have totally misrepresented the event, and then spend the majority of the time trying to convince them to follow Christ. Now don't get me wrong trying to convince students to follow Christ is awesome, but misrepresenting an event is not cool. For one thing kids will spread the word to avoid going to future events due to their experience. I'm not saying you shouldn't include fun in your meetings. Or that you need to divulge every minute of what will happen at a youth event in promotional material. I think you probably understand what I mean.

Here is an example: I was part of a group of youth leaders who brought in a Christian speaker to the area. He had an awesome story and was a great communicator. I had no problem being part of the event. He laid out to us exactly what would happen at the school assemblies and at the end of the week when was doing an evening production at a local school. The assemblies went as expected and a ton of students showed up for the evening meeting. Once this guy hit the stage he did nothing that he told us he was going to do. He had promised the teenagers a certain kind of production and then didn't even come close to delivering it.

What he did that night was to put on a Christian rally with old style fire and brimstone preaching. He was accusatory of the kid's behavior without knowing any of these students or if they were into the stuff he was referring to. They thought they were coming to an upbeat event with a funny speaker (like he had been in the assemblies) with prizes and a rock band, etc. However, none of that happened. I was embarrassed to even be a part of the event. As a result I'm very careful now as to what kind of events I participate in. Nothing can kill your outreach quicker than for word to get out that you're part of a "bait and switch" ministry. Teens are fine with us laying out our case for Christ as long as they don't feel deceived or manipulated

Here is what we do at our weekly outreach meetings. We meet from six to eight pm. To draw students we put up posters and post online highlights of the excitement and energy of the night. When the kids get there those are the things we do for the majority of the night. We spend no more than twelve to fifteen minutes laying out our case for why we follow Jesus, giving them one piece of the puzzle of who Jesus is. Some of the staff have had a hard time with that because they think in a two hour period we should have been spending more time talking about Jesus. But by giving them one piece of the puzzle kids are intrigued and look forward to learning more about who Jesus is. They begin to put the pieces of the puzzle together and the full picture of Jesus emerges. Then they can begin to decide whether or not He is someone they want to follow.

Someone who is seeking truth is like a plant growing out of the ground (Mark 4:1-8). There is nothing we can do to hurry up the growth in a healthy way. Even giving it too much water will kill it. We need to water and nurture it, giving it just the right amount of nurture and sustenance for it to grow in a healthy way. People seeking the truth need enough information to keeps them interested in looking for more, not to feel pressured or overwhelmed by our efforts.

Or course it's much more convenient for us to get 150 teenagers in a room and pound them with the truth. But I believe it's more effective to take time with students, learning where they are coming from spiritually, and giving bits and pieces of information about

Jesus as they experience life. At the same time compare the truths of God with what they are currently going through. That way they experience Jesus as they experience their life and it becomes more real to them. Their faith in Jesus is more likely to grow and strengthen for the long haul.

Carole's Note

Reach out to the teen girls. Learn who they are. Find out where they are coming from. What are their sorrows? What are their joys? As you get to know a person God will give insight as to the best way to share the Gospel with them, and it is rarely a fire and brimstone presentation from stage.

Chapter 29

You are Endorsing Whoever you put on Stage to speak to the Teens

As I shared in Chapter twenty-six when it comes to inviting others to your events you have to know when to stand your ground and be true to what you know about working with searching teens. You will find there are people who will try to pressure you to do what it is they think you should do. You may hear, "you should ..." from parents, people in your church, relatives, and other people in ministry as well. Sometimes I think it's from a pure motive. But other times it's a manipulative kind of thing. Sometimes when people can't draw students to their approaches they try to attach to a ministry that's doing well. They want to push an agenda through your ministry.

In my early days in ministry I was more easily manipulated. I thought everyone had better ideas than I did so I was willing to go along with many things that I wouldn't touch today. People talked me into having guest speakers, for example, who seemed very sharp but later I'd regret having them involved. I began to realize how much the teens depended on me to put someone of quality on stage. When a guest was on our stage the students assumed I was endorsing everything they said and did.

On one occasion someone told me that a certain rapper would be a great addition to our weekly production. So I had him come, do some rap songs, and tell a little of his story. At first the students were into his music but then I could see them starting to get bored with it. At one point the students began talking amongst themselves. The dude stopped his rap and started yelling at them, saying that he had the stage and they were to respect and listen to him. He also started doing promos for places where he was going to be performing, which included bars and clubs. It was great that those venues let him perform as a Christian artist but it would be inappropriate for these underage teens to go see him at those places. So I learned the value of vetting someone before I put them on stage and giving them clear guidelines for what was appropriate to promote or speak about from stage.

Not long before this writing, a long-time friend came to me at church and told me about his son who had just been released from prison, had become Christian, and speaks to youth in group settings. I had spent a lot of time talking and listening to this friend of mine as he told me about the problems that his son was causing, which eventually ended with him in prison. While he was incarcerated he became a Christian, and now that he was out he wanted to help teens avoid the mistakes had made. His father has become his agent contacting churches, youth groups and school, trying to get his son speaking gigs. After being burned several times over the years in these types of situations I told him that since his son just got out of prison I would like to see how he does in life for a while before I put him on stage speaking to the students at our youth program. Of course my friend was insulted and we haven't spoken for a while.

When you are selective and careful about who you include in your ministry you are going to offend someone. Count on that happening and remember who you are protecting. Do the vetting yourself, learn from experience, ask a lot of questions, and make sure they follow your agenda when at your events. You are responsible for what these students see and hear. Don't be afraid to say "no" or "not right now." It's okay if they get mad. You're making the right decision, in the right way, and for the right reasons when you're looking out for your students and are concerned with their souls.

Carole's Note

Others will come to you and try to enlist you in changing your husband's mind. If you have important information about someone, share it with your husband privately, but be united with him in public. If you disagree with your husband's decisions, discuss it when you are alone. The united front is very important to a strong marriage, and to a strong ministry.

Chapter 30

The Underrated Ministry Tool

One thing I've noticed in youth ministry (and this goes with anything involving people) is that everyone loves it when food is involved. It even changes the dynamics of a situation. How about "Hey everybody, we're going to clean the youth room." The kids go "Oh man, why do we have to do that?" Then you say "I'll go get pizza so we can eat while we clean." Attitude change!

I believe food is an underrated ministry tool not used to its potential. When you look at the Bible Jesus used food as a ministry tool on a number of occasions. There was the feeding of the 5,000 (Matt 14:13-21) and the feeding of the 4,000 (Mark 8:1-9) for example. When someone is fed a basic need has been met.

There is also something disarming about food. When you're sharing a meal with someone an air of openness seems to develop. If I am having trouble with a guy in our youth ministry I'll meet him for pizza and we'll spend time talking. Usually, when separated from the rest of the group, and feeling comfortable with some pizza in front of us, we can get to the bottom of what's going on. My wife can accomplish the same thing if the situation involves a girl. And the students involved will talk about that time together for years.

When we have any kind of a meeting with students and/or staff we have food. It seems to make for a much more relaxed meeting. I believe we get more accomplished with everyone feeling nurtured, open, and secure.

With our youth ministry schedule we alternate from week to week with a large meeting one week and a small meeting the next. Our smaller group times consist of students who are more interested than the general population in growing in Christ and is called C.O.R.E.(C.O.R.E. is explained in chapter 10) And at the core of our meeting time is dinner. We all share a meal together for the first third of the meeting time. We just eat, hang out together, and table talk. It's a very valuable time. On the weeks when we have our large group productions we provide dinner for the staff because many of them come to the ministry right from work. Again, we try to meet a need with food. There are many people who love projects and providing food for a group is definitely a project. We have couples on our board of directors, small groups, family members, and others who provide a meal or two per semester.

This is something I feel is very important. If I meet with a student or an adult I always want to pick up the check. If I'm meeting with them there is something I want accomplished in the relationship or situation. A meal is a small price to pay. The guest feels cared for and that you're investing in your relationship with them. Especially if I am meeting with one of my volunteers or students they will never even see the check, that's how fast I take it. Food! An awesome ministry tool.

Food can also be used to further relationship building. I will give a couple of examples. Often when I visit school campuses I bring a pizza or two and sit with some students that attend our youth program. In every school lunchroom is at least one person I refer to as the "lunch scrounge." He or she (usually a he) spends two thirds of their lunch break going around from student to student asking for spare change for lunch. One such lunch scrounge noticed I brought in pizza for some students and hovered around our table. I watched to see how his lunch scrounging unfolded and it didn't look like it was going so well. He finally gave up and sat at the end of a table, half-heartedly engaged in the conversation with students around him, mostly looking out the window. Along with pizza I had brought a two liter of pop and some cups. So I put a couple of pieces of pizza on a plate, filled a cup with soda, and took it over to him. When I set it down in front of him he looked at me and said, "Why are you doing this? What do you want?" I told him there were no strings attached and I hoped he would enjoy the pizza. Then I left.

The next week he was at our youth program. He was a little stand-offish at first but he kept attending and slowly began to warm up to people. Eventually he became a Core student. He even went on some extended trips with us. Years later I was visiting the school and chatted with the principal. He told me how that young man had changed for the better. He had become a Christian about a year into attending our youth ministry. Two pieces of pizza and a glass of soda started that process. Great investment!

In another instance, one night after a board meeting Carole and I decided to stop for dessert. We were sitting at a booth talking with an older couple that had just finished their meal. I looked across the room and noticed a student that attended our youth program and his female friend. The boy came running over to us, giving Carole and me a hug. He told us about what was going on in his life.

We asked him about his church and he shared he was tired of the church judging him for being gay. I know there are two sides to a story so I'm not making a judgement on the church, but obviously he was bothered by how polarizing this subject has become. After talking with him for a minute I noticed his female friend patiently waiting for him to leave. So I waved her over and she introduced herself. After talking for another minute I reached over and took their bill. She asked, "What are you doing? Does this mean you're paying for this?"

I told her they were our guest and that we would pay for their food. She asked me why I would do such a thing. After all, she and this boy are gay and we are Christians. So I shared that for many years we had been on the other side of life where we didn't have much money and people would pay for a meal, blessing us in that way. Now that our situation is different we in turn wanted to bless them. She responded that she wanted to check out our youth program. Another victory for FOOD!

As I said, providing food, or picking up the tab for someone's meal, can open up ministry opportunity. It's a moment that can slip past us so my suggestion is to re-think the use of food as a ministry tool.

As I shared, when we first started ministry we had very little money. People usually ended up blessing us by paying for our meals. You may be at that stage in life yourself. Just let other folks bless you. There will be a time in your life, later, when you will be able to pass the blessing on to others. When it happens it will be a joy for you because you will remember how you were blessed by others in that way.

Carole's Note

Our oldest daughter Angela calls food "hugs in a bowl." When we deliver a meal to a sick or grieving person we are offering a hug. When we serve a meal to a teen it shows we care about more than just having another kid in a seat at youth group. So keep those pots and pans busy! Recruit friends and family to help. Bring them into the ministry in a unique way!

Chapter 31

Make yourself Indispensable

My first gig was a combo job as a junior high director/janitor. One of my former youth pastors told me, "Make yourself indispensable." He planted that nugget of advice as I was complaining to him about the janitor part of my work. He told me to do a good job with both. But then be such an awesome youth pastor that the church would eventually say, "Why in the world are we wasting his time with janitor work? Let's hire someone else for that and let Dave work fulltime with our youth!" I agree with my friend's premise to make yourself indispensable. However, if I did it over again I wouldn't complain about the janitor part. I would do both to the absolute best of my ability so the church would think that if times got tough I would leave such a huge hole both in the janitor role and the youth position that they wouldn't want to lose me from either.

As far as youth ministry and the duties it entails its true you will in fact be a janitor, babysitter, cook, taxi service, errand runner, bookkeeper, accountant, advice giver, listener, and most of all, a servant. Make yourself indispensable in every part of youth ministry. If the church ever gets to the point of needing to reduce staffing they will prioritize keeping you because of the plethora of things you do in a top notch manner.

Carole's Note

Your job as a wife to Mr. Awesome might mean you are included in that long list of job titles he has. Your help in any area possible will get him home to you all that much sooner, and that support is a bonding tool for your marriage. Being committed in that way is a service to not only the teens and church, but also to God. It is a ministry. And might I add that on top of the list for you is to be his encourager. It doesn't help anyone for you to nag or complain or to be angry with the work load the church gives your husband.

But if they are truly expecting too much of him speak up! Kindly and professionally bring it to the attention of your husband, the church board, and pastor. The place to bring the issue to light is not through complaining and whining to members of the church. The outcome will be much better if you work as a team and handle any overload in a professional manner.

Chapter 32

Teenagers know when they're being Played

Early in my youth ministry days we were living in Durham, North Carolina where I was working for Youth for Christ. Our YFC youth ministry was drawing students from a couple of schools in the area. The schools were open to us visiting campus so I routinely would eat lunch with some of our students each week. As I was standing outside of the cafeteria one day, I invited on of our students' friends to attend an upcoming event. In response he said, "I've been watching you and I don't think you really care about us. I think this is all about you. I think you're just trying to build your little youth group empire."

At first I was insulted. I'd given my whole career to helping teenagers. But the more I thought about it and analyzed my motives, the more I came to the same conclusion that he did. He nailed it. I *was* somewhat motivated by my competitive nature and wanted to have a larger youth group to brag about.

His unsolicited comment changed my approach to the work. I decided I needed to care more about students than about how I look to other people or other groups. I shared with the students who were at the core of our group that I was no longer going to talk up the ministry to them or their friends at school. I shared my desire to be motived more about caring for students when I visited the schools. I told them that if this ministry was going to grow it was up to them – I was no longer going to be a promotions guy. My focus would be caring for them and their friends.

My role as leader of the ministry has become one of caring for the students first and foremost, and making sure that if they were to invite their friends to our youth program it would be a great experience. They would never be embarrassed to bring their friends.

In other words I want them and their friends to walk away each week feeling that coming to our meetings was worth their time. I wanted them to leave feeling loved, valued, and safe.

Now when I go schools I talk with students in a way that's all about showing them genuine interest and concern. I leave the promotion of the youth ministry to those that are already involved in it. When a student at the school says, "Hey aren't you the guy who runs the M.A.D. House teen program here in town? What kind of stuff do you guys do" I connect them with a student that is already involved, and ask them to share about the ministry with the inquiring person and invite them to attend a meeting. I want to make sure that my motive is right and students know it.

Carole's Note:

It's hard for a guy to keep things in balance. Their career and ministry can become their identity. As his wife do little things to remind him of who he is, apart from being the guy who runs that super youth group. Hold each other accountable for keeping life real, balanced, and motivated by the right things.

Chapter 33

Watch your Life Gauges: Mental, Physical, Emotional, Social, and Spiritual

Decades ago I heard Bill Hybels teach about keeping our eyes on life's gauges. I thought it was one of the most profound ministry maintenance tools I'd ever heard about. He related our personal life to gauges in a car and taught us how we need to keep monitoring them.

I've always owned an older car. My first car in high school was a 1962 Chevy Impala. Now granted, the year I owned that car was 1972. Since then I have always owned a 1960-something Chevy. In those days cars had very basic gauges for gas, oil pressure, engine heat, and alternator. You have to keep your eyes on the gauges to monitor that the needles are within the safe zones. When one of them gets out of whack you need to take care of it. In the case of a car fluid levels need to be adjusted or something needs to be tightened to keep it running well.

In life, and especially in ministry, we also have gauges that we need to watch in our lives. Just like the car gauges, if a needle from one of them goes out of the safe zone we have to make a correction.

Early in my youth ministry career I was really feeling down, to the point that I wasn't sure that I would be able to stay in that job. I remember calling some friends for advice to see if they could diagnose why I was feeling this way. I thought that if I was staying pretty physically fit, got plenty of rest, and my spiritual life was strong, I should not be feeling the way I did.

At the time I was preparing for an event where I was to speak. Looking up passages in my Bible I came across this verse: "And Jesus grew in wisdom and stature, and in favor with God and man." (Luke 2:52 NIV). The scripture was about Jesus' growth between the time he was twelve and when He began his ministry, and it is the only verse that really gives us insight into Jesus' life between those times. It said that Jesus grew spiritually, socially, mentally, emotionally and physically.

God used that passage to reveal to me that I have more than spiritual and physical gauges in my life, and they all needed to be monitored. I learned of three more. Mental, emotional, and social wellbeing also need to be healthy and in balance. Even though I was keeping up on my spiritual and physical wellbeing I was struggling in other areas. How were my mental health, attitude and mind being strengthened? What about my emotional health? Was I was internalizing things that were negatively effecting my emotional wellbeing? Last but not least was my social health. Were my relationships with my wife, students, and kids healthy and balanced?

We all need to keep our eyes on the various gauges of ourselves as we go through life and ministry. These areas also interact with each other. If one part of us needs correcting, another area will be affected. Bill's advice was simple. Just as we keep an eye on the gauges of our car so as not damage it we need to watch our personal gauges to make sure we don't burn out or destroy ourselves, and perhaps others around us in the process.

I have often heard and witnessed the truth of the statement that it takes a lifetime to build a good reputation but only one moment of indiscretion to lose it all. Keep an eye on your gauges to protect from that.

Carole's Note

Add some fun to his life … and yours! The fun part of monitoring and evaluated your life gauges is that you get to take time to recalibrate. You have to care for yourselves. Have a get-away planned now and then. It gives you both time to check your gauges, give attention to any necessary adjustments to your life, and to reconnect with each other. Include these times of retreat in your budget. It could be an overnight, a week, or even just an afternoon. One of our favorites is to slip away to Lake Michigan to float in the water and just talk things out. Find out what recalibrates you!

Chapter 34

Every Ministry Needs a Hugger

This tip may seem small, or even silly, but it is actually huge. As I deal with kids, being a guy, I have a tendency to be right brained, dealing with life more analytically. If someone needs information, a problem fixed, lecture given, or issue analyzed, I'm your man. However, when it comes to feelings, emotions, and touch not so much. (Refer to Gary Smalley's book *Keys to Loving Relationships*)

A few years ago a student from a local high school died in a traffic accident. Many kids involved in our youth ministry knew and loved this person. A year later we were on a trip with some students 1,500 miles away from home when the one year anniversary of this student's death came around. Being the analytical, right brained one, I missed it. My wife and a couple of the students went out to the beach at night and had a little service of remembrance. When they got back, being the *sensitive* one, I asked what was going on and why two of the girls were crying. My wife reminded me of the anniversary of their friend's death.

I didn't know what to do to comfort the girls so as they sat on the porch and cried I made some popcorn for them. I know it sounds silly, and probably was. My analytical mind came up with the idea that food can be comforting. But of course the reality of the need was that my wife's loving hugs and comforting touches got them through this ordeal. Every ministry needs at least one hugger. When there are no words coming and there is nothing you can do to help, a hug comes in pretty handy.

Hugs are also a way that students repay or console staff when they are going through tough things. When my wife's dad died we were in one of our youth meetings and she began to cry. She was sitting off to the side out of my direct view so I didn't immediately see what was happening. All I saw was a student walk across the room in the middle of the meeting, right past me, over to my wife. He got on his knees so he would be eye level with her as she was sitting down and wrapped his arms around her. Then another student walked over, and another, and another. Pretty soon all of the students were in a line waiting to hug my wife. Of course my prepared teaching stopped as the lesson being taught by the kids was much more relevant and powerful.

But remember to be sensitive and careful as you dole out the hugs. It's generally more acceptable for women to give both the teen girls and the guys hugs than it is for male staff to do so. So give hugs out very carefully and appropriately. Good side hugs or a pat on the back are ways we guys can appropriately offer comfort.

Carole's Note

Physical touch is important. It can also be unwanted, in cases of abuse or neglect. You can tell if you try to put your hand on the shoulder of a teen who has been abused. They may pull away or even get angry. Keep that in mind. And as a woman remember to make the hugs appropriate. No matter your age you have body parts that can be a disadvantage, if you know what I mean! Be aware. Be appropriate. And keep an eye on others as they give hugs. Be on the buffer between a hug being a ministry tool and being the end of a ministry career.

Chapter 35

You Can Love the Student and Hate the Behavior at the Same Time

I think one of the hardest concepts for young people (and probably some older people) is that of hating the sin but loving the sinner. There isn't a verse in the Bible that makes that precise statement, but it's the way Jesus worked. Since we look to Jesus as our model it should be the way we work as well.

We had a real shake up in our ministry that involved college age students that we called associate leaders. The label came from the fact that they were in the process of changing their associations. They were beginning to associate themselves less as high school students and more as adults. As one of these associate leaders began to demonstrate some very poor choices I had to ask him to step down as a leader and basically leave the group. He had tight relationships with some of the students and they were very angry that he was asked to leave. But it really wasn't our option to kick him out – he violated his contract with us. The agreement included the expectation that if he broke the contract by specific behaviors he terminated his own leadership involvement.

I did my best to explain that to the students. As weeks went by the young ex-associate leader came back to us and apologized to us and to the student body. As far as the kids assumed that was that. The end. They thought this associate leader would be back in his role at the next week at our meeting. When the next week came and he was not there students began to ask about him, so I explained he was not allowed to come back. The students were shocked. They thought that the apology would resolve the problem and put the issue behind us all. I tried to explain to them that to forgive does not always mean to forget, which is what they thought. They wondered why, if I forgave him, I wouldn't let him back to his original position. But this person had violated the trust of a student and he violated his own oath of leadership for the ministry. We forgave him but he would not be back in a leadership role. His act had consequences. We love him but we hated what he did. And though this person was forgiven, trust was a step that needed to be dealt with.

This is a huge lesson for students to learn as they get closer to God, learning more about his nature and how he operates. God loves us even more than we love ourselves, but he also equally hates our sin. He is loving and He is just. These profound qualities can be illustrated to the students as we deal with issues that come up in ministry.

The truth of hating the sin and loving the sinner is more relatable when you have middle school or high school age children of your own. I really began to understand it as my children grew into their teen years. They began to spread their wings and yearn for freedom. They began to make their own choices in friends and activities. As kids grow the troubles they can get into grow as well. You will love your kids until the end of your life. At the same time you will understand that when they do something you fully and completely hate you will still fully and completely love them and that love will not waver. A good youth leader can carry that concept into youth ministry.

Carole's Note

Back your husband up. You know what I mean.

Chapter 36

Know where Your Responsibilities End

The kind of kids we work with in our ministry are at risk teens, meaning they can be real trouble sometimes. Add to that the fact that we are living in an era when students often aren't held personally responsible for things they do. People tend to want to blame an organization or someone other than the student for their behavior. And I found that if I wasn't careful outside problems would become the problem of the youth ministry.

Here's what I mean. Let's say a couple of students are dating and come to our youth program together. Then the couple finds out they are pregnant. Because they come to the youth program together the people involved try to make it our problem, like we should have somehow prevented it. I communicate to them that while I agree there is a problem, it's not a youth group problem. The problem was caused by the choices of two students. I won't accept the blame for our ministry.

Let's make up a situation and unfold it. An example would be two students who were dating and both happened to attend out ministry. They were at a party and the boy tried to aggressively push the girl into having sex with him. The party is in no way connected to the youth program. Students and adults alike may tell you about what happened, and because the students involved are part of your program, ask you what you are going to do about it. There might be comments insinuating you are somehow to blame for the issue. Some of your leaders may even fall for the idea that the youth program is somehow responsible.

I'm in no way suggesting that we would refuse to help in some way, or that we shouldn't get involved at all. In fact, laws are in place that require us as leaders to report certain incidents when we have firsthand information. What I want to make clear is that although students may at times have a personal problem, it's not a youth group issue. It's a result of individual choices. Coming to grips with that has helped me avoid carrying the stress of believing that poor choices kids make are my responsibility or within the boundaries of our work.

Again it comes down to knowing where our focus must be. We need to stay focused on what God has clearly called us to do. We can protect the youth group, but also get involved with helping the teenagers who are involved in the crisis. We can walk students through situations, getting them the help they need. But it's strategically important to your own peace of mind, and to the image of your youth ministry in the community, to know where to draw the lines between individual and group behavior. When this concept is clear in your mind as well as understood by the other leaders you are prepared to face this type of challenge.

Carol's Note

Over the years we have had to make tough calls to Child Protective Services (CPS) or to the police, and while it's never easy it is vitally important that you know your responsibility as an adult leader working with minors, and follow all laws regarding reporting incidents involving youth. You can check with the local police, school officials and child protective services to get correct information and guidelines.

As a leader of a youth ministry we must not allow these types of incidents to override the ministry. If a situation arises where police need to be called to the scene send a trusted volunteer out to meet them so it doesn't distract from what is going on in your program at that time or cause unnecessary drama.

When a teen is in danger of hurting themselves or others, make the appropriate calls. But if you merely hear a rumor that you can in no way substantiate keep your eyes and ears open and do some extra legwork to verify if you should do something to help defuse a bad situation.

Another important aspect of this responsibility is that as adult leaders working with youth we need to earn trust. We should think twice before calling police or CPS any time we hear about issues but there is no known danger or law breaking. If we make those calls needlessly teens will believe they should keep their problems to themselves. They won't reach out and ask for our help.

It is a fine line to walk but the well-being of the teen, your volunteers, spouse, and the youth group as a whole is worth the extra effort. When you do turn a student or a situation in to the authorities, it is very likely that your relationship with them is over. Don't let that stop you from making an appropriate report. However, be prepared for a broken relationship with a student who may learn you reported an incident involving them to authorities.

Chapter 37

Conflicts with Church, Neighborhood, Police, School, Parents will Never Stop

I used to be really bothered when we experienced conflicts with people in the church or the neighborhood, or if we had to deal with police or local businesses because of something one or more of the students had done. We could have an awesome night with the students and then one thing would happen at the end of the night, a complaint or a problem of some sort involving someone from the community or the church, or the police would stop by, and it would ruin the whole night for me. I would even lose sleep over it for the next few nights.

I yearned for being able to have youth meetings that would go smoothly. But inevitably, a few students would cause problems and the complaints would come rolling in. I even found that kids from the neighborhood would misbehave and our youth ministry would be blamed for it. I began to get complaints when our kids were just standing around doing nothing wrong. People from the neighborhood didn't like the fact that they were standing around, even in our own parking lot, because they looked like "trouble".

I came to a few decisions that made it a lot easier to live with these types of ministry challenges.

1. I took responsibility for incidents that were our problem, but stood my ground when they were not. I found that people would push me as far back as I was willing to go. Now, when someone comes to me from the neighborhood and complains that the kids look intimidating while standing in our parking lot I

stand up for the kids. On one occasion, a local business shared the parking lot with the church and their customers began using the area of the lot designated for our group. Then they complained to me because they were afraid their cars might get damaged on our youth group night, even though it had never happened. The business people had plenty of parking they could use but they chose to park where they knew the kids were going to be. When they called the church to complain about something that *might* happen, they were shocked when instead of knuckling under to their complaint I suggested they park on the other side of the parking lot, closer to the business. How dare I stand up for the kids instead of adults running a respectable business? But they did start parking back on their own side of the lot and the positive result was that our club kids had more room to park on meeting nights

2. I realized that if I wanted to have a ministry to at risk teenagers peripheral conflicts are going to happen. No matter how hard I tried to set things up so that tensions were avoided, I was not going to be able to prevent all conflict. Once I realized that's the way it would be I had to decide if I could live with those conditions of ministry. If not, I should get out.

If I could tolerate it, then I would settle my mind and let God help me deal with it. Most of all I need not to worry, although I admit I do sometimes. I think about this scripture: "Do not be anxious about anything, but in every situation, by prayer and petition, with thanksgiving, present your requests to God. And the peace of God, which transcends all understanding, will guard your hearts and your minds in Christ Jesus." (Phil. 4:6-7 NIV) Most of what happens we can't control, and most things we spend time worrying about don't happen anyway.

3. We decided that a couple of times per year we would thank some of the local businesses that had to put up with things relating to our ministry. Here are a couple of examples. Periodically our staff and kids go out and pick up garbage in their lots and around their buildings. There was a McDonalds near one of our bus stops. The kids would hang around inside, order little if any food, and just be loud and obnoxious like teenagers can be sometimes. We had the kids sign a card to thank them for letting them hang out inside during the winter months as they waited for the bus. The students delivered the card to the manager with an

enormous box of candy, flowers, and a hug from each student, thanking her for her patience with them. She was very excited. Sometimes little acts of gratitude go a long way.

Carole's Note

We have some power to step in before problems arise. As ambassadors for the ministry we can defuse problems by personal interactions with businesses around where we meet. Visit and thank them for their kindness to the teens they might encounter. Offer a bit of insight (nothing personal) into the lives of the teens and why this ministry is important to them. Include the community in the process. Offer praise to them for any good they do, like supporting local school functions. I even go so far as to bake cookies and put a note in thanking them for seeing the value in our work with the kids.

Chapter 38

Helping Teens Go on Trips and Events

If you're working with teens and reading this, you probably will do almost anything to enable certain kids to participate in a trip or event. Of course we want them to benefit spiritually, but there is also an element of life experience that goes along with them become well rounded adults. After all, the kind of adults we become is basically an accumulation of our life experiences. So we want to give the students as many positive experiences as possible.

As you continue your youth ministry you will find yourself focusing in on certain kids that you would like to see benefit from trips or events your group is doing

In my early days in youth ministry, the group I worked with would travel to Gatlinburg, Tennessee where we joined up with about 1,200 students from other areas. We really pushed the kids to go on this trip. We did sales, car washes, and other fund raising events so as many as possible could go and participate. No matter how much money we raised it was never enough to send all of them. But it would be a great life experience for them, and there was a huge spiritual opportunity for them that could never be duplicated at home.

Some of the students seemed a little indifferent about going, and I thought if I could get them there, they would most likely connect with Jesus, coming home a different person. Sometimes that happened and sometimes not. But I was determined to get them to join us. If, after all the fund raising, there still was a shortage of money I would come up with money somehow. Carole and I would even save money through the year so we could pay for some of the kids to attend.

Because we used a good portion of own resources helping kids participate we ended up having to buy loaves of bread, peanut butter, and jelly to put in my hotel room. I had no money to spend on fast food.

On one of these trips I remember making my way to the arena for the evening meeting. I walked past a very nice and expensive restaurant. At a window booth sat a group of my students. The same students I helped by personally working hard and saving funds all year so they could attend the trip. They were having a great time eating lobster and steak. I learned they'd come with hundreds of dollars in spending money. And on top of that they pretty well blew off most of the ministry I was hoping would effect and impact them spiritually.

After that hard lesson I changed my strategy. I focused on students that really desired to attend and required that they make some sort of an investment in helping get themselves there. Usually there was some sweat equity investment involved where they had to participate in a fund raiser. But they also had to pay some cash toward the expenses. Even if they participated in a fund raiser there was extra value to them if they paid personal funds as well. I find kids seem to take the event more seriously if their own money is on the line, and it offers them some personal dignity as well.

So much in our society strips people of their dignity. People will gladly take what's free, but what they don't realize is that in the process their dignity is being slowly eroded away. I would rather not play a part in that. The combination of sweat equity and the requirement of some financial investment in order to participate with the rest of the kids on a trip is something they can feel proud about. Mission accomplished!

Carole's Note

We can get a good feel for who needs help the most if we talk with parents and teachers of students. Who really needs assistance, and who is just playing us for a free vacation? Do the research. It's worth it. Not every teen will benefit from every event or trip so try to be selective. Keep your eyes and ears open, and pray for wisdom. Then give freely, and with joy!

Chapter 39

Repeat After Me: "I Don't Know."

As professional youth workers we feel we need to have the answers to every the question that teens throw at us. In our ministry we get hundreds of questions from kids about God and life. And many are good, well thought out questions they sincerely want answers to.

Part of our weekly production involves small group times that we call Break Out. We do some high energy stuff during the evening, which include skits, games, live bands, multi-media, and a challenge. The challenge involves a ten to fifteen minute time slot where we try to get the students to open their minds to thinking about God and how He could fit into their lives. After the challenge we have Break Out. We sort the kids into small groups, making sure that a team of staff members and regular attenders are in each. They are given questions based on the challenge that are designed to get the kids to dig into their lives and see where the information fits. The small group time is purposely designed to get a discussion initiated about the night's topic, which makes the kids think and helps them retain the information longer than if they just heard it and went home.

One thing that's been crucial in facilitating a successful discussion is that the staff don't see the questions until the night of the meeting. That's important because if the staff get the topic and questions ahead of time they do a bunch of preparation and instead of there being an opportunity for honest discussion and sharing, the students will get what amounts to a Sunday school lesson.

As a result the staff's number one complaint has been that they weren't able to research and prepare for questions they expected students to ask. They were basically embarrassed that they had to say, "I don't know the answer to that question."

Repeat after me, "I don't know." It's alright to admit it. In fact, it creates an opportunity. "An opportunity for what?" you might ask. It creates a ministry opportunity, maybe like no other. I have taught our leaders to be honest with students when they don't know the answer to a question, assuring them they will do some research to get answers. Then the leader suggests having lunch with the student so they can talk about what they find.

This response tells the kids that: 1) You don't think you know everything, 2) You respect their question enough to take action, and 3) You value them enough to not only spend time doing research on their question, but also to spend personal time with them.

The fact is the follow up ministry time will become so valuable you will hope they ask more questions you don't know the answer to.

Carole's Note

Within any group of ministry volunteers there will likely be a variety of biblical backgrounds. What one might know another has never studied. Lean on each other to help in answering kid's questions. Involving other staff in growing your understanding of something not only shows respect to the volunteers, but also helps kids realize how many people care about them.

With internet and phone use so readily available we often go home after a meeting and message teens later in the night or over the coming days. We give them a link to a website with answers, insights we found later, or send a Bible verse that God led us to showing them we are thinking of them long after the club meeting. It also provides opportunity for further contact.

Joyfully, I can share with you that I have been able to lead numerous teens to Jesus through our texting times! Teens are often more vulnerable, able to focus, and have extra time needed when they are at home alone, able to put their jumbled thoughts into a text or an online message.

Chapter 40

Make Contracts with Your Leadership Students

As I sat across the table at McDonalds talking with one of the students involved with our ministry, regardless what I said, this person just kept asking the same question, "Why are you kicking me out?" No matter how much I tried to explain to this student why they could not be part of the student leadership of the program they interpreted my words as them being kicked out of the group. From their perspective, it wasn't that they violated the important guidelines of being a student leader, but that I was mean and had no mercy. Through this experience I learned a very important concept: a person's perspective is their truth. It doesn't matter if it's the real truth; their perspective is what they've decided is *the* truth. As this student went on to talk with other kids, "Dave kicked me out" was the headline of their story.

After this happened, and tired of having a false narrative out there, I decided to document some things. The result was a contract between our youth ministry and any students wanting to become a leader. There were three parts:

1. Purpose statement of the ministry
2. A detailed job description outlining student leader behavior expectations and responsibilities, including penalties for not following the rules of the contract.
3. A statement that if they violate any of their responsibilities, or if their behavior becomes a problem, they have chosen to remove themselves from student leadership. A place is included for them to sign and date the contract.

By having the job description and signing this contract we are assured that the students are aware of their specific responsibilities. We go over them in leadership meetings a few times throughout the year to refresh their memories and provide an opportunity for me to point out anywhere they are failing to comply. When and if they fail to hold up their end of the contract, they have removed themselves from leadership. Dave did *not* kick them out.

The student leader then has a choice. They can work with us to recommit, making the adjustments necessary to remain in a student leadership position, or they can choose to rescind their contract and remove themselves from the role. Of course, there are instances where the offense calls for immediate removal. But usually it will be a behavior that can be changed, resulting in growth for the leader.

If a student chooses to drop out they have to sit out at least a semester before they can be considered by staff for return to the leadership role. This process helps us avoid a lot of conflict and hurt. It can also be used to refocus a teen where they need to grow. It's a great tool to use for protection of the whole group.

Carole's Note

If you have a good relationship with a teen who is having issues following the rules of the leadership contract take the heat off your husband and, if possible, step in to deal with that student. Whoever has the best and most positive relationship with the teen should be the one to lovingly guide them through the process. Also, never allow a volunteer to hold this over the heads of teens, constantly threatening them with being kicked out. Your husband has the final say in situations like this. That's why he gets paid the big bucks, right? ☺

Chapter 41

The Least Likely Thing Can Be a Strength

A pastor friend called to pick my brain for ideas for a youth ministry. He said that some teenagers from the area had been coming to his church for a bon-fire every Saturday night. The community where he ministers is known for having a lot of teenagers who cause trouble around the neighborhood. He'd become acquainted with a few of them who started sitting around a campfire outside his church on Saturday nights. The group grew to about twenty teenagers. But the problems began as teens were getting rowdy and fighting at the get-together.

I asked him who helped him with the group. He told me that it was only him and twenty teens. He said it had gotten so bad that he'd had to end the gatherings for a while, hoping it would break the cycle of fighting.

A couple of older ladies wanted to help, and his wife said she would come, but they had a handicapped child who would have to attend as well and he didn't want to do that. He also didn't think the two older women could relate to or handle the teens.

This guy approached his life and work from a standpoint of strength. He felt the need to appear strong to those around him, and he carried this idea into his work with the teens. I told him I thought he was working with the teens from a misconception. Those two women, his wife, and his handicapped son could be his best assets. If teenagers understand anything they understand vulnerability. They deal with it every day of their lives. And when they were around this strong pastor their guard would go up. He appeared to have no weaknesses, which was of course not true. The truth was that he just hid his weaknesses well.

I suggested he ask the two older women to come to help. His wife could also be an asset, especially with the vulnerability of his son. The walls that the teens come to the meeting with would melt away and his group would transform into something that he never imagined.

Sometimes I think we look so hard for the answers to our youth ministry problems when the solutions can be right in front of us. Before you look far and wide for things that can help make your ministry strong, look right under your nose. You may have overlooked something.

Carole's Note

A few years ago we were blessed with a grandchild born with many health issues. She was on a ventilator, a feeding tube, and so much more. We were care-givers for our precious TaNyia when her mom was at work. The time came when our ministry schedule collided with our daughter's work schedule. What could we do? We decided to bring her along to the meeting.

That was a turning point for the months ahead. Teens fell in love with our sweet girl. Some would come and ask to hold her, and even learned a little bit of her care so they could help. As they would reach out to TaNyia, we got to talk. We shared how God sees our needs, and how our faith in Him grew through the experience of having TaNyia in our family.

There were teens who accepted Jesus because of our little miracle girl. And when she passed into heaven, hordes of teens attended the visitation and funeral, witnessing the celebration of her life. More teens accepted Jesus.

Was it easy to bring her to meetings and retreats? No. The packing alone was a huge undertaking. Keeping her away from germs while in public was always a concern and took extra time and care. Was it worth it? Absolutely, every bit! And there are young Christians looking forward to seeing TaNyia's precious face in heaven someday, people who might not have made a decision to follow Jesus if they hadn't met her.

Chapter 42

Nurturing Your Volunteer Leaders

In our youth work we have been able to keep many of the same volunteers for decades. I found that's not something that just happens. Youth work, especially a ministry to lost or at-risk teens, is very hard on volunteers. It can be time-consuming and the teens can be very challenging to deal with. They will drain leaders physically, mentally, emotionally, and spiritually. The secret to maintaining volunteer staff involves a thought out and purposeful approach.

Most of our volunteer leaders have been with us for ten years or more, and a number of them have been with us for over twenty years. We've had very few volunteers who quit once they got hooked on the ministry and the kids. This is our approach:

1. I ask them to sign a contract that will take them through one schoolyear. Once we've vetted them through a screening process, they commit to one full year of ministry. That gives them an out at the end of the year if they want one. There is no guilt if they decide not to continue for another year. During that year we also see who really has a heart for working with tough teens.

2. We prioritize assuring they are growing spiritually. Each time we're together we try to get some spiritual growth into our meetings. I like to put in something that is personal for them as individuals, as well as material to help them be more effective in ministry with the teenagers.

3. It's important to make sure they aren't letting the kids overwhelm their time. We never ask them to give up important family time. I've made some significant mistakes in that area myself. In supporting our volunteers I go with my gut. If

something is not right I respond to it instead of just letting the feeling pass. There have been times when I've felt the kids were overwhelming staff, resulting in too much time given to the ministry. Staff are in danger of neglecting other personal priorities such as time with their spouse or their kids. Over time I saw this happen with some of our staff and realized I had a responsibility to step in. Their home/ministry balance was off, and their family was suffering because of it.

Here's an example: A very sharp person joined our team. I knew the students would love him and be drawn to him. He was a spark plug type of guy. He dove into the work full force, and after six months I became concerned about how he could be involved so deeply, and at the same time spend adequate time with his family.

Along with my gut feeling we noticed vibes coming from his wife. When we were around her she seemed distant and not enthused about his ministry involvement. Eventually I asked him about it and he assured me she was totally on board. So I let it go.

As I think back, my quickness to drop the subject probably came from the fact that he was such a great volunteer leader that I didn't want to lose him. I was putting the ministry's needs before those of him and his family. Another six months passed and he came over one day to tell me his wife had left with his children and was filing for divorce. Remembering my earlier concerns about the situation, I realized should have reacted to what I saw. I should have been more persistent in inquiring about the issues troubling their marriage and family. But I didn't follow my gut and pursue my concerns about his volunteer time with us. It very well may have contributed to the divorce. If I had decided to tell him to take a break from the ministry and reconnect with his wife and children it could have made a difference. To this day, I regret I didn't do that.

4. Hold volunteers to scheduled time off. Living in Michigan our yearly schedule is very seasonal. It's easy to divide up the ministry schedule to assure that staff have ample time to be away from ministry for rest.

Here is how we divide up our year:
*Late August: We begin to regroup the staff after the summer (meet for three weeks)
*Mid-September: We begin to put our Core Students and staff together (meet for two weeks)

*Late Sept. or early Oct: We kick off the ministry

*November: Take one week off for Thanksgiving

*Mid Dec-first week in Jan: We give the volunteers time off for Christmas break

*Mid Jan: We meet with Staff and Core Students

*Last Week in Jan through the first week of April: Meet from kick-off to spring break

*After spring break we meet through the middle of May

The volunteers take the summer away from the ministry for the most part but there are a couple of events we gather for that are fun and spiritually profitable. Volunteers have a choice about whether to be involved in these events.

The volunteer leaders burn hard ministering to the students a total of about nine months per year. I want to make sure they stay in balance, with plenty of time away from the kids to help prevent burnout so they are excited to be with the students when they are with them.

5. Care for your volunteer staff in other ways like sending cards, letters, and online messages. Take them out to lunch and never let them pay for their meal. If you don't have the money personally, put it in your ministry budget. You won't regret it.

6. Model ministry for them by being a servant. Carole and I try to be models to the volunteer leaders. This means doing things for them and with them. I always want them to be able to take advantage of time with the students. After our youth meetings I usually begin to do a little clean up. As the volunteers see me do that they pitch in and begin to help, but I tell them I don't want them to help because it's their time to spend with the students. Their response will often be that they don't want to leave my wife and me with the mess, but I assure them that the mess is our job to clean up and their job is to connect with the teens while they are there. Carole and I have times outside of club night to connect with the teens. The students want and need club night time with the volunteers. It's still hard to get good leaders to stop cleaning up because their desire is to do anything they can to help. Over the years, as we've gotten older and it's more challenging to do all the physical work, we've recruited volunteers solely for the purpose of set up and clean up. These volunteers excel at it and see it as a ministry, which it really is!

7. At the end of each school year we celebrate. We host a volunteer appreciation dinner complete with gifts and added words of thanks. It's more than worth the money and effort to show appreciation for these precious people.

All of these efforts combined add up to caring for the volunteers so they are able and excited to be a part of the ministry. In our case, most have lasted between ten to twenty five years serving the Lord in this ministry.

Carole's Note

Effective and long lasting ministry prioritizes volunteer care. Inviting a few volunteers over for dinner now and then can be more than just a nice gesture. It is a way to keep tabs on the well-being of your greatest ministry assets. The side effect of this is building lasting friendships. We have enriched our lives beyond belief through the friendships we have built with our volunteers.

Many times a volunteer will come to us with ideas of extra things they want to do with teens. Picking teens up for church on Sundays, having a bonfire at their home in the summer, or a short term Bible Study. We question them to make sure they understand the time commitment and risks involved. We also want to confirm that their enthusiasm and ability are up to the task. Nothing can hurt the morale of a group faster than starting something and then having the ball dropped. They should be able to execute their project without your help so your time is not stolen away from other needed areas. Then if you can join in it is a bonus, not a necessity.

Each situation is unique. One volunteer might have hours upon hours of free time they want to use for ministry. Another might only have barely the two hours a week available for the club meetings. So be aware, be encouraging, and be in prayer for them through it all.

A good approach is to treat your volunteers the way you would want to be treated. It's biblical! Take time to volunteer for something just for the experience of being in the volunteer role. What did you like about volunteering? What didn't you like? How can you use that experience to make your volunteers feel appreciated and useful?

Chapter 43

What about Using Parents as Volunteers?

About thirty years ago we had a trip planned with our youth program. So many students wanted to attend that we realized we were going to have a transportation problem. A few parents came forward and offered to give rides to the event, which involved spending the night at a hotel. Being as desperate as I was I accepted the offers of a couple of parents who had mini-vans, which would be a huge help. The event seemed to go well. We went to our destination, had a great time, and returned home safely.

The next day I got a call from one of our volunteer leaders. She told me that one of the parents had alcohol in their van. No one saw the parent drinking and I didn't smell it on him. We all got there and back safely with no other incidents happening that drew my attention.

However, it made us re-evaluate some things. We had "dodged a bullet" with this event and we wanted to make sure we were more careful about who helps with activities. A parent might seem like a good idea. But unless you know them well you can't be sure what their motive is, or the kind of person they really are. People are very capable of putting on a good front. I know I may sound like a cynic, but protecting the kids needs to be a high priority for any youth ministry. The conclusion that we came to after that experience was to only use parents as volunteers if they have gone through the application process and have been vetted properly. I know this isn't convenient at times. But it only takes one poor decision to destroy a life, or bring down a ministry. We owe it to the students to do everything we can to protect them. They and their parents put their trust in us.

Carole's Note

You also want to check with your ministry or church to see what their policy is, what insurance coverage there is, etc. Think through each decision before you make a final plan. We're aware that you can get so cautious in decision making that the ministry comes to a standstill. If that is the case, re-evaluate policy. Recruit more volunteers. Choose other activities. Whatever it takes.

Chapter 44

Give your Volunteer Leaders Authority along with Responsibilities

One of the most frustrating things about volunteering in any group is to have responsibilities without any authority to make decisions. When a situation arises, the volunteer has to run to the leader every time he or she is faced with a decision because they don't have authority to make the call on their own. This is one reason it's important to vet the people that want to volunteer for your ministry, spend the time properly training them, and then trust them to make decisions.

When volunteer leaders first start working with our group we ask them to check with us before making a decision on something related to the teens. At the beginning of a volunteer's involvement with your group they may lack the confidence that they will make the right decisions in certain situations, or the experience or knowledge to do so. We counsel the leaders to tell students that they will give it some thought, or check it out, allowing them time to talk with leadership about the situation. The volunteer and the leader can make a decision together.

With time and training the volunteers get more understanding of, and experience with, the ministry. And we become more confident of their judgment and abilities so we can give them authority to make decisions along with the responsibilities they hold.

On the other hand, you might have volunteer leaders who feel they can make decisions for the ministry on their own before they are ready. You will have to troubleshoot and put out some fires. You may need to spend time with that leader individually to explain some things. If you do it over lunch, just make sure that you pay for it. Before getting to the concern, spend time encouraging and building them up. They will likely leave feeling it was a positive experience.

Carol's Note

Even married couples won't see eye to eye on every issue. There will be decisions your husband makes that you won't agree with or even like. It's important for you and your husband to show a strong front together for the sake of the group. The youth pastor has to be the final say in youth group decisions and situations within the youth group. There will be times you disagree. Don't do that in front of the kids. Pray, take time after the busy night is over and discuss it rationally and with respect and kindness. Maybe the youth pastor…your husband… will see it your way! Maybe you will see it his way. But the main thing is, stand together in front of the teens if at all possible.

Chapter 45

Spiritual Growth of your Volunteer Leaders

When a volunteer is involved in youth ministry with us we have an opportunity to make a real contribution to their spiritual growth. Every time we get together with our leaders we have a devotional to feed them spiritually. It could be simple or a more interactive production, but there is always something. At each meeting we have with the students I also try to include things in the devotional that volunteers might not know, or something that will help them as they minister to the students.

We've had certain volunteers around specifically because they need personal spiritual growth. Serving is a great spiritual growth tool, stretching people in a way that nothing else can. Volunteers have to dig deeper to find answers to questions the teens put forth. As they deal with the kid's spiritual needs they confirm for themselves why they believe the way they believe. Working with the kids as a volunteer forces them to pray deeper, love harder, and give more.

One final thought I'd like to add to this section is that nothing is more powerful than modeling ministry as a lifestyle. People watch what you do much more than they listen to what you say. We try to be inspirational to the volunteer leaders through our actions. Everything we do in the ministry we do for God and we try to make that show through commitment, excellence, and service. Our actions may speak more to helping the leaders grow spiritually than anything that we say to them.

Carole's Notes

Keep your eyes open for needs not only in the teens but also in the volunteers. Your ministry is as much to your volunteers as it is to the teens. As you help them grow they will in turn be able to minister to the teens more effectively, and the ministry will flourish.

Chapter 46

Volunteer Training

There is a lot to know about working with teenagers. Not everyone is aware how teenagers think and operate. We work hard at keeping up with kids as society changes and people change with it. We keep the volunteers up to speed on all of that information as we receive it. Training is a never ending, on-going effort that happens all through the years. There are some things that we repeat over and over, every year, because they are so important.

One example of that is what we call our listening tool. It's a one page training tool we use to teach the staff how to effectively listen to students. It describes how to give advice when it's asked for, but most of all how to ask the right questions of students as they deal with their issues so they can be sure they made the right choices. The questions are designed to help the student work through challenges in such a way that they can came up with their own answer. When they came up with the answer on their own, it's more likely they will follow through and take the actions required.

Part of caring for our volunteers is to assure they are adequately trained and feel competent and up to date. We make sure they take time off, away from ministry and teens. We treat them as equals and friends involving all that goes with friendship. We value their opinions and ideas, assigning them into positions where they know they are contributing something important to the ministry. We spend time telling the group about the value of each of them and even try to meet some of their physical needs. One way we do that, and the thing I want to spend a little time on in this section, is the use of food. When you provide food or share a meal, good things happen. Walls come down, it feels like a family, and volunteers know they're being cared for.

We were fortunate to have an amazing cook offer her services to our ministry. Two Thursdays per month we have our large group outreach. The other two Thursdays, just the volunteers and Core students (those students in our discipleship group) attend our gathering. At the Core week meetings our wonderful volunteer cook provides supper for everyone – students and volunteers alike. For the large group weeks, because some staff have to come to the ministry site right from work, she prepares meals for the volunteers. Of course some of the Core students get in on that as well. If a student comes without having dinner we offer something to them. This may sound like a minor thing, but I as I shared earlier, food is an underestimated ministry tool that makes people feel loved, cared for, and breaks down walls.

Carole's Note

For this part of the ministry, I recruit others to help as much as possible. When the woman mentioned in this section moved away we continued the food ministry. At the beginning of each semester I send out an email asking for volunteers to feed the masses. I ask board members, friends, relatives, and church groups if they can provide a meal. Often these people bless us by taking more than one meal and will feed us multiple times! Others will combine with someone else to cover the meal needed.

We keep it simple: chili and cornbread, or hot dogs and chips might be on the menu. Other times it gets very special, like full turkey dinners for Thanksgiving, or a sit down fancy dinner hosted for Christmas. The teens and staff love it all. It is another way to get people involved in the ministry as well. The people who provide meals often end up thanking us for letting them attend and see the group in action.

Chapter 47

Using Anticipation to Keep Kids Energized

Early in our youth ministry, some of my students would come to me when the school year was almost done and ask, "Why do we have to stop our weekly meetings? Can't we go through the summer and keep meeting?" The first few years we did that. And guess what happened. The students who consistently bugged us about continuing the program through the summer stopped showing up after a couple of weeks. In fact, a few weeks into the summer almost all of the students stopped attending. In our area, summer is a different kind of animal from the rest of the year. Summer jobs are plentiful. It's one of the few times it is warm enough to be outside for long periods of time. I learned my lesson. Now when students beg us to continue our big weekly production through the summer we say no.

But we didn't want to squelch the kid's interest in the program so we started using their excitement to the advantage of the program, using the tactic of building anticipation. We would end our club meeting in the spring on the biggest note we could. We made it extra fun, exciting, and very high energy. We would then let the kids know when we would be kicking off in the late summer and wished them a great vacation time.

Throughout the summer I would give them little bits and pieces of the things we were going to do during our fall kick off. I found that a summer away from the weekly ministry production, along with some teasers through the summer, is a good combination for building anticipation on their part. Then, after being apart from the ministry for three months, they are ready to go and will commit to attend for the full school year. Can you imagine football or basketball or any other sport for that matter, going year round and never ending? It wouldn't work. The excitement and anticipation of the next season energizes interest in both the players and the spectators. What makes it special is that there is a season for it. A beginning and an ending. You have to wait awhile for it to come around again. We try to use that same anticipation to energize both the volunteers and the students for the coming season.

Even as the season grows close students and volunteers will call us to ask when we will be beginning the weekly ministry productions. By the end of the summer they all seem to be chomping at the bit to get started. Again, we stick with our kick off date, no matter how much prodding and begging that comes from the staff and students. We send them information about what's coming up and try to build anticipation and excitement for the big kick off. I caution though that there is a window of opportunity where you can use anticipation and excitement for ministry advantage, and when that window passes, loss of interest is a danger.

So use the tool of anticipation wisely and sparingly to help your ministry grow. Anticipation can be your best friend to keep the spark in your in work. And always leave each week with both the students and the volunteers wanting more.

It's not that we don't have any contact with students over the summer. We do. Some of the leaders do as well. It's just not the big weekly productions in the style that we do during the nine months of the school year.

Carole's Note

Use down time to double up on small group gatherings, one on one appointments, planning, fund raising, and rest. These are all very important parts of a ministry and need attention as much as anything else.

Chapter 48

Teens won't always speak up for themselves. They will just disappear.

Some years ago we started attending a new church in the area. There was so much energy and excitement for this adventurous start-up church. The congregation met in a number of places before finally purchasing its own facility. The reason for moving around was because the new church kept outgrowing the buildings places it rented.

Carole and I volunteered to help with the youth program temporarily until they were able to hire someone. We didn't have the time needed to continue with it because we were already working full time in a teen outreach ministry. For a short time the church was meeting in a school gym and the teenagers would stay in the main service for the praise and worship time, then go into another room for the teaching time. As we were leaving the gym with our medium size youth group the little children were leaving at the same time, a much larger number than the group of teens. I remember the pastor commenting about how huge the youth group was going to be when the little kids became teenagers. Meanwhile, I was thinking, "Yeah, if that's actually how it worked."

Younger kids are a much different animal than teenagers. When your kids are little they go where parents tell them to go, eat what their parents tell them to eat (well, sometimes), do what their parents tell them to do, and believe what adults tell them to believe. If you go to church it's not an option for your little children. If parents go they bring their little ones. But as kids grow and become pre-teens they might start questioning and maybe even put up a fight about attending church. When they reach fourteen or fifteen, some parents give up the fight and let them stay home or sleep over at a friend's house.

Teenagers get a mind of their own and begin to question the validity of church and Christianity. They don't want to believe just because their parents believe it. This is when it takes a real focused effort to keep teens involved in church. Church isn't just about God stuff. Church involvement teaches us about community and all that goes with it. Kids gain skills and understanding they will need as they enter society on their own, as adults.

We developed the youth program to keep the teenager's attention and keep them wanting to come back week after week. To some adults the style of a ministry geared to teens is annoying and obnoxious, and they wonder why it needs to be that way. "Why can't you just sit around a table nice and quiet and talk about Jesus?" they ask. "Why do you need to entertain, and be loud, and make messes with food?" And the people in a church who think that way are also aggressive in trying to put a stop to it.

Here's my example for you: I was working at a church that had a missionary from Africa speaking during mission week. The missionary was dressed in African clothes, played African instruments, sang African music, and provided some African foods, and the people in the audience were excited to tears. Meanwhile, outside in the field next to the church we were having an outreach event for teenagers. Everyone was dressed in teenage style clothes (jeans and t-shirt), playing teenager style Christian music, eating teenager type food like pizza and hot dogs, and having a great time. Some of the same people who were praising the missionary for doing the exact same thing we were doing outside came out and tried to shut us down.

I find teenagers are often pretty timid. If someone with a strong personality declares their point of view, often teenagers will not come back with a strong response. They may not like or believe what they hear but may not be able to come up with a concise response. They will just walk away and later complain to their friends about what they heard or how they were treated. Putting this in the context of a youth group, a teenager who gets turned off will just leave. You may never know what happened because they won't let on that anything is wrong. They just won't come back to your youth group and that's the last you will see of them. You may never know why they're gone.

The point I'm trying to make here is that you need to make sure you're speaking up for the kids. They will not speak up for themselves. I've worked in a few churches where we needed to fight for having the style of ministry we knew would draw teenagers and keep them. You will need to decide how far you can go with that. As you look for a church in which to work it's important to know if your passion and style is compatible with that particular church.

One of the churches I worked for decided they didn't want the style of youth ministry we were bringing. They got a new youth pastor. When we left the group there were seventy teenagers attending regularly. After two years with the new youth pastor there were four students attending the meetings. Because we attended the church, Carole and I were asked to step back into working with the teens. We did so temporarily, and immediately came against resistance as our ministry style drew teenagers, but brought conflict with some of the church folks. The youth group had built back up to having dozens of teens.

I believe anyone could have done what we did if they were willing to stand up for the teens and for a style of ministry that would keep teenagers interested in being involved, while learning more about Jesus. There will be times you need to stand up for the kids, because they won't speak out for themselves they will just disappear.

Carole's Note

On the other end of the spectrum you may have teens who come for fun and games and nothing else. They might be attached to influential families. You again need to stand up for what is right. What is going to get God's Word to the most teens in a way that engages them and helps them come to a decision? Spend time talking with the board members and pastors to show them the validity of what you want to do. Your way might not be the only right way. You may need to compromise to fit into the church you are working for. Whatever the case, speak up. Speak for yourself, and for the teens.

Chapter 49

Lines should be Drawn Where They Are the Clearest

People love to use precedent in their favor. In fact, our laws here in America are built on the precedent of decisions from previous cases. This is especially true for teenagers. They love to find loop holes in things that they want to do but are told they cannot. Being pretty tender hearted towards teens, I like to give in, give them the benefit of the doubt, or give them extra credit. I like to make exceptions for them. However, my generosity in making an exception is often used by the student against me later. "Why can't I? You let me do it before!" Or "You let them do it, why not me? It's not fair!" And the place they ask me those questions is in front of a whole group of their friends. So now I've compromised myself on a rule and made that rule very muddy. I've also made it harder on the other leaders to deal with that rule. "Remember way back when Dave let us get away with that? If you were as nice as Dave you would bend the rule for us too."

Now I'm not saying that we never bend the rules for kids, because we do. I put more value on a teenager than I do a rule. However, bending the rules is a very tricky thing; it needs to be done sparingly and with careful thought. I have explained to other students why I bent the rule for a student and they're usually pretty understanding. They recognize that I was valuing the student more than the rule.

Having said all that, we've made a policy in our ministry that we make rules sparingly and the ones that we do make are very clear. We try to draw the line where it is the clearest.

Here is an example: For years we struggled with whether or not we would let students continue to come to our high school ministry after graduating high school. It's a critical time for a young person's development emotionally and as a Christian. At first we would let them continue to be part of the high school ministry for one year after graduation. That grew to two years. Then they started bringing their college age friends and the problems began. Guys in their twenty's trying to date girls who were fourteen and fifteen years old was not a good or safe situation. Parents definitely weren't on board with what was going on.

So our policy changed. When teens graduated from high school they moved on in life. But as usual, teenagers surprise me, even after forty plus years of working with them. When students dropped out of school, went to adult education in place of high school, and drew it out beyond their projected graduation date, they expected to be allowed to attend the youth program.

The line that I thought was clear had now been muddied again. Our next and final attempt to draw a clear and defining line was this: The summer of their eighteenth year, which is the time they should have graduated, is the end of involvement in youth group.

To ease the pain and misconception of them feeling kicked out, whether they officially graduated from high school or not, we have a special graduation ceremony to mark their departure from the group. We give them gifts and have a great time sending them on to the next phase of life. We also allow them to come back and visit one time per semester so they don't feel ex-communicated from us. And they have total access to Carole and me, as far as continuing to help them and communicating with them. We've become their friends, and sometimes they feel like we're family. We want to make sure they know we are still there for them even though they've moved beyond being a student.

Carol's Note

We make sure the graduation ceremony is very special. They get a unique t-shirt, candy, and a devotional book. We have a "gauntlet of hugs" as volunteers stand in a line and hug them when they walk down the aisle. We make sure the weeks and months after graduation are peppered with cards, emails, or Facebook messages, invitations to church meetings, and special outings with other new graduates, etc. This is a tough transition time for many. They still need us.

Chapter 50

Most Lessons in Life are Caught, Not Taught

Once a week, Carole and I buy some pizzas and go to an alternative high school for lunch. We meet with ten to fifteen teens. This special high school is for students who have a hard time making it in a main stream school for a variety of reasons, mostly due to behavioral issues.

Here is the problem that we sometimes face. These students function best when there is a constant routine. However, because their personal lives are often in chaos it makes routine at the school nearly impossible. Many students miss a lot of school through the year. Consistency in anything is pretty much out the window. For example, if a kid and I are having a great discussion and the bell rings signaling the end of lunch time I can't suggest we pick up our conversation the next week, because next week many of the students won't be there. Continuity is a big issue. Change is constant. With these students the tough issues they are facing can change from morning to afternoon.

Another issue is that the lunch time is only twenty minutes long because if these students are given too much idle time, big problems will result. During that twenty minutes of discussion students may be called down to the office, there may be a fight that breaks out in the hall, or the police may show up for something. A student or two in the group may have had a terrible week, acting out and spurring drama, and on and on it can go.

With all of this stuff happening, we felt like we were spinning our wheels and not really making any kind of a difference in their lives. I mentioned that to the principal one day after an especially bad lunch meeting with the students. I'll never forget his response. He told me not to underestimate what the students were learning from us. He said that every minute we spent with them we're teaching them something.

I began to take notice some of the things they had learned. When we first started meeting with them they would come into the meeting and just tear into the food, not really caring about anyone except themselves. So we started teaching them some manners and respect, both by speaking it into their lives and leading by example. We also would ask them for permission to ask blessing on the food. They were okay with that. During the blessing, I would take my hat off. One day I set up the lunch and had to run out to my car to get something. In the meantime the bell rang. When I got back to the room the students were all at the table with their heads bowed, hats off, and one of them was thanking God for the food. Not only had they patiently waited before digging into the pizza, they prayed and even removed their hats, which I never told them they had to do. I had just removed mine to set an example.

We realized then that we were teaching these kids important qualities like consistency, manners, respect for others, and how to interact with others appropriately, to name a few. What else could they be taking from this time together and applying to their lives?

We still have meetings that are depressing to us and I have those fleeting thoughts that we are spinning our wheels. But I always come back to the principal's encouraging and truthful words. Every minute we are with the students, we are teaching them something.

Carole's Note

During those short little meeting times, we might only get one small nugget of the Gospel out to the students. Over time, there is enough information for them to make a decision to follow Christ. Every minute given is worth it.

Chapter 51

Volunteers Are Just That - Volunteers

Have you ever been in a situation where you were counting on volunteers to follow through on an assignment for an all important event, in which they played a key role in order for it to be a success, and they failed to follow through?

If you are a paid staff in a youth ministry you are considered the "hired gun." Volunteers know you're the one who gets paid for doing the nitty gritty work. Therefore, you have much more at stake in the ministry or in an event than a volunteer leader ever will.

I've had events where a volunteer didn't show up and didn't call to let me know. I would say to myself, "Well, I'll just put Joe in the place that John was supposed to be" only to discover that Joe didn't show up either. Cue chaos: shifting staff around from this place to that place. Most of them do not have the gifting or talents to be in those areas left empty by their fellow volunteer who never showed.

So I decided to become learned in many things. A youth leader has to wear many hats from bus driver, to toilet cleaner, to cook, to web designer, to teacher and disciple maker.

I made the decision that I was not going to be put into a situation again of patching in volunteers to a task they didn't know. I began to expand my knowledge of all the tasks, at least enough to get us through the crisis. I became pretty effective at running sound and lights, developing a power point production, cooking, web design, and many other tasks. I even went through the training and licensing process so in a pinch I could drive the bus if I needed to. And all of this knowledge has come in handy from time to time.

Some professional youth workers may think what I've shared here is a bunch of hog wash, and that I'm just not good enough in the arena of training and developing my

119

staff or I wouldn't get into these situations. That may be true. I can always get better at training, developing, and motivating my volunteers. But I'll stick with my theory because you can train and develop and motivate your volunteers to perfection, but there are still going to be times when they are sick, or have family issues, are on vacation, or had to take another shift at work. I love to learn anyway so getting moderate experience with a number of ministry tools is something I love to do. It also makes me more valuable and experienced to an employer, so it's really a win all the way around.

Carole's Note

There are club events when we are missing most of our volunteers. What can you do as a wife in these situations? Scramble! What can be knocked off the schedule? What areas can be combined to take fewer adults to oversee? Most of all, don't panic. Don't bad-mouth the volunteers who are not in attendance. Praise the ones who are there and build them up.

Keep an eye on the volunteers for hidden talent that could be pulled out some night when needed, thus showing that volunteer that yes, they are good at filling that empty spot!

Chapter 52

People Love to win Things

As my children were growing up, we would make tons of trips to Chuck E. Cheese. Why? Partly because we love pizza. But another reason was the games and prizes. We would always order the pizza packages including crazy amounts of tokens. When those tokens were spent we bought more. Was it all for our kids? Absolutely not! My wife and I loved to play the games and win prizes too. I have to admit I probably loved it more than my wife because I am goal oriented. I had my eye on a prize and would play as long as necessary to win that prize. And the prize? Well, we could have probably gone to a store and bought it for a tenth of the cost but it was so much fun trying to win it. Yep, that's it; people love to win stuff.

Many years ago we decided to put that philosophy to the test with the students. Here is what we did. We took our Core students and attached points to everything they did connected with the ministry. Every time they showed up for the weekly meetings they got points. If they brought friends they received points. They gained points for attending church, for memorizing the weekly verse, and triple points for writing the verse out with their thoughts about what it meant. They earned good behavior points, which were subtracted if they messed up. A point system is also a great way to build your groups attendance. If we wanted more kids to start coming from a certain school or age range we would put a bounty on those students. We would raise the points very high for those teens we really wanted in attendance.

Here is how we structured it:

Attendance each week:	5 points
Bringing friends:	1 for each friend
Friends who returned:	5 points for each friend
Memorizing Verse:	5 points (teens who are not part of our Core group could learn five verses and earn a t-shirt
Writing Verse/Meaning:	15 points
Event Points:	5 points (Dressing up for Halloween event or the Hawaiian luau … etc.)

Each point is worth ten cents of credit to spend within the ministry. Here is how the points could be spent:

- Purchase at the snack bar (candy, pop, t-shirts, etc.)
- Free entry to large events like our Battle of the Bands Rock Show or other concerts we sponsor.
- Part of the expense for a trip or event
- Purchase of food for the annual Core student retreat when they are required to pay for food.
- Toward the cost of a friend attending an event.
- If your youth program is blessed with funds you could even do things like turn points into cards for gas, fast food, or other creative stuff kids can use.

Our Core students can also spend points to regain a missed attendance point. We allow each Core student a certain amount of absences. If they go over that, they are dropped out and have to sit out a semester before returning as part of Core. Some students don't take attendance seriously assuming they can just jump back in the next semester, which is why we kept track of their absences. So if they go over their absences allowed they can spend points to buy back one attendance miss. The price is high so they don't want to miss many meetings.

The final thing they can spend points on is the end of the year auction. Some students will spend their points throughout the year, even buying stuff from the snack bar for their friends each week. But since we began our auction they've been much more careful with saving their points.

Here are a few things that we auction off at the end of the year:

- A day tubing behind a boat on a local lake along with a steak dinner cookout.
- Canoeing down a river with some volunteers and kids.
- Dune buggy riding for an afternoon.
- Pontoon boat ride out on a local lake with a pizza party onboard.
- Tickets for a local Christian music festival
- Gift cards from stores and gas stations
- An afternoon of pizza/video gaming/go cart riding/mini golf.
- T-shirts, hoodies, jackets, hats etc., with our logo.
- When there are prizes where four or five can participate other students can buy into the event if they have enough points.

The point system is an effective behavior enhancer. If staff see a Core student misbehaving or causing problems, like talking during a meeting time, distracting others, they can take ten points per incident. You will be amazed how a system like this will work to refine the behavior of your student leaders.

The points will even help keep their social media on a more positive track. When students want to join the Core one thing that is considered is their social media behavior. I let them know if I don't think they can be a part of Core based on junk they post on Facebook. I am amazed at how quickly it's cleaned up if they are really motivated to be part of our Core group.

I find a point system very helpful for building positive things into the teens' lives as well as ejecting negative behaviors out of their lives. In fact one local school found out about our point system. A teacher and a principal asked for our information because they felt something similar would work in their school. A great tool for helping shape behavior!

Carole's Note

Volunteers have wonderful ideas! How would they like to spend time with teens? Roller skating? Baking cookies? Frisbee golf? Whatever they enjoy I can guarantee there are teens who would enjoy spending time with that volunteer, involved in that activity. Encourage each volunteer to think of ways they can spend time with teens, maybe in groups. Two or three volunteers can offer a prize together. Whatever they decide, make sure it is safe for all involved and that they follow through with the student who purchases what they are offering.

Chapter 53

There are Two Sides to every Situation

You can really get yourself into trouble by not knowing all aspects of a story. I've created a lot of problems for myself and for others when I took a side in a dispute before knowing all the information from all sides. Even though there may be only two sides to a debate or argument, there is peripheral information other people have which is good to know.

For example, two students may have a big disagreement causing tension not only between them but also others around them. Getting information from other friends or family members (possibly about something that's going on at home) can give great insight as to why one or both of the students are acting the way they are. My theory? Don't be afraid to ask questions. Try to get the full picture before making a decision about what to do to resolve the situation if it's necessary to step in

I can't tell you how many times I've had teenagers talk to me about friends, or more often parents, or something going on in their home When a student is at odds with their parent(s) they try as hard as they can to get people on their side. As they try to lure me into believing their story I say, "You know, there are two sides to a situation. I don't want to make a judgement on something until I hear both sides." Then they usually say, "You think I'm lying. You don't believe me!"

My response is: "Yes I do believe you. I believe that you believe that you're telling me the whole story. But if there is anyone else involved, there is another side to this story." They usually continue to try to make me understand that they're giving me the full picture. But I stand by my decision that though they may think they are telling the whole story, they can't possibly be doing that.

Speaking from experience with my own teenage daughters, it's easy for people to get sucked into a story a teenagers is telling. When I had to discipline one of them I would get calls from other parents telling me that I am a terrible parent and how dare I do this or that, or talk to my daughter that way, or be so mean to her. I got thinking that if my own children can make someone believe something about my wife and me other teens could do the same about their parents, or about a Mad House situation.

So do yourself, the teen, and all parties a favor and gather all the information you can before coming to a conclusion. It will save you some heartache and some embarrassment, and help you make a better intervention into what's going on if that's required of you

Carole's Note

The times we have sought out the full story have been used by God to bring others to him. One particular teen we worked with in the past often shared with us how bad her life was at home. She was perpetually depressed and often suicidal. I spent hours listening to her as she poured out her pain and depression, getting one side of the story. We've experienced that frequently a teen will embellish their stories to get attention, find affirmation, or just to get more time with a leader. But in this instance as I learned more from her sister, her mom, and her dad I found that the student had genuine reasons to be depressed and wanting to give up on life.

Years have passed, and as we've learned more about this young woman's life we've been able to reach out to the whole family. She has learned all she needs to know to make a decision about Christianity. And so has her family. Her sister accepted Jesus and is praying for her atheist dad and her depressed sister. Her mom became a friend of mine and finally let me in on the secret that she accepted Jesus into her life, despite the fact the her husband has forbidden it

Chapter 54

It's not Always important for Teens to know what we've done for Them

Sometimes you'll know the right thing to do, but because of the situation it is better that no one knows what you did.

Let me clarify. Over the years we have helped students in many different ways. Some were small gestures and others not so small. Like giving a student one of your cars, or putting on an open house for a senior student at your home, which we've done a few times.

In the case of the open houses we provided all of the stuff that a high school graduation open house needed for a couple of students. They each put a box out for people to drop cards and money in. Halfway through the day I looked in both boxes and noticed that one was getting full and one was empty. One of the students had many family members stop at the open house and the other invited just friends to come. And though friends are nice to have around they usually don't give money at an open house. They just eat sandwiches.

So I went to the bank and got as much money out of my savings account as I was allowed, leaving the minimum five dollars in there to keep the account open. I purchased envelopes to put some of the bigger bills in so it would look like adults had put thought into their gift. I also used smaller bills, crinkling some to make it look like teenagers had thrown money into the box. When the day was over both students went to their boxes. One student was excited because he knew that his box was going to be well stashed. The other student more hesitantly approached hers. As the student picked the box up her facial expression showed she was surprised by the weight of it. When she emptied it, quite a bit of money dumped out and she counted it excitedly, exclaiming "Do I have great friends or what?" To this day, after years, this person still doesn't know anything about where that money came from. The student had a great day, she made a great haul, and believes she has great friends.

Carole's Note

It's ok to keep a secret – that was some of the best money we ever spent.

Chapter 55

The Relationship Bank Account

Our ministry is relational based. I came across a theory from a book called *Keys to Loving Relationships* by Gary Smalley, and immediately it made total sense to me. It describes something that happens all the time – Gary just brought it to our attention. Relationships are like bank accounts. Let's say you have money in a savings account. You continue to add to it. And every once in a while you need to withdraw some for a particular reason. Sometimes the withdrawal is for a vacation, but more often than not it's to pay for a car or house repair you're unable cover with your paycheck. So the money comes out of your savings account. If you continue to withdraw money without putting money back in, eventually you are going to end up not having enough for an emergency

Relationships are like that. We invest into someone's life day in and day out, building the relationship. Inevitably something negative happens, drawing on the relationship we've built. But as long as there are more positives than negatives the relationship will stay healthy.

Here is where the problem lies as it relates to youth and their parents. Some moms or dads don't have a positive balance in their relationship account with their teens. Most of their interactions are negative, so the relationship depletes, just like the savings account with a negative balance. When one reaches that point even good moments can't pull the relationship back to a positive place. Everyone feels like they are walking on egg shells because a look or a comment can take a potentially positive time and turn it negative.

We've had times like that with our own children as teenagers. Sometimes we chose to let some behaviors go when we wanted to react because of the negative effect it would bring. We were careful to pick our battles and bite our tongues when we wanted to speak. By doing this we were able to avoid draining the relationship. If the relationship bank account gets very low it may take years to build it back to the point of having a healthy positive relationship with a teen. But it's worth the effort. We prayed that God would give us patience and a fierce love for our children as we were trying to rebuild the relationship bank account. This also applies to the teens that you are working with in ministry.

Carole's Note

My rule is to put more in than I take out. If you know you have to deal with a tough situation with a teen, make sure you build up that account before, and after. You need to discipline a very poor behavior and you know it will cause pain and a rift in your relationship? Say and do some things that will bring joy and help them feel loved and affirmed.

Some of my favorite ways of building up teens: Sending notes in the mail. Snail mail means love. You put time and effort into it. Writing a Bible verse that shows them they are loved by God is always a good choice. Other ways to build up the account are by taking them to lunch and let them pick the place, hugs if they don't mind that sort of thing, even giving them the left over cookies after club! Any little thing that shows you are thinking of them and care about their well-being is an addition to their account. Then when you have to point out a negative behavior, they respect your input into their lives because they know you care.

Chapter 56

When are you too Old for Youth Ministry?

When I got into youth ministry at twenty years of age I didn't give any thought to how long I would be able to be sustain it. After all, what young person looks that far down the road? We are consumed with things that are going on in our lives in the moment. We're never going to be old!

I don't know if age and ministry really crossed my mind until I was creeping up on forty years old. As I was staring forty in the face, for the first time I wondered how much longer I would be able to continue in direct ministry with youth. Sure, I could probably do some support youth ministry. After all, I would have twenty years of service under my belt. I could maybe be a youth worker supervisor or office support staff. But how much time did I actually have left with direct youth ministry? How much longer could I be the cool youth guy, as opposed to being seen as a youth worker has-been, just trying to keep up appearances? And how long would the teenagers accept me as a youth director? Is there an age when being a youth leader becomes "creepy"?

Then, something happened as I turned forty that I think happens to everyone as they get older. The age you thought seemed so old suddenly doesn't seem that old when you get there. It's like we expect that when we hit certain ages a switch is going to go off, and suddenly we officially feel and act old. Instead, I felt the same as I did when I was twenty. I could still relate and connect with teenagers, and they seemed to more than tolerate me. They seemed to still love and accept me like they did when I was in my twenties and thirties. And I enjoy ministry more than I did when I was young. It's meaningful in a deeper way.

Then I realized something else. Teenagers don't see age as much as they see love. In their need for love and acceptance they seemed to look right past my age and right into my heart. They knew that I loved them and accepted them unconditionally, even if I stood against their negative behaviors.

And now, as I am in my sixty's I am enjoying youth ministry more than ever. The motive is different, the advice is different, the hugs are different (it's more like a hug from a grandparent) and definitely the energy is different. But as long as I can keep up, and God will use me, there is nothing else I would rather do with my life.

An interesting side note: We took a couple of vans full of the students from our youth ministry to observe another group. On our way back, we asked the students what they liked and didn't like about the way that group operated. The one unanimous critique they came up with was that the group didn't have enough older staff! Half of our staff are now over fifty years old. Don't think that you are ever too old to help in a youth ministry. Teens see your heart, not your wrinkles.

Carole's Note

Age can be an asset in youth ministry. As I have aged my ability to speak to teens has grown and deepened. I can "get after" the kids and get away with it. Kids see me as a loved grandma. They want to please me and I can use that as an advantage. I can have heart to heart talks with them, pointing out things that are disturbing in their lives. They might only listen out of courtesy for the old lady, but they have heard it, and the Holy Spirit will use my words for his good.

A hug from a grandma is a good thing. A hug from a twenty five year old woman can seem sexual or wrong. I love being older in youth work. It opens doors that were not there when I was younger. An added blessing is seeing teens step up to help me because I am old. I no longer have to lift heavy boxes or carry things up and down stairs. Teens rush to help me. And my gratitude to them warms their hearts and adds to that bank account we were talking about!

Chapter 57

Culture Change and Ministry

We have seen a lot of things change in American culture during our years in ministry. The decade of the seventies had its own issues. As the decades changed, so did the nature of the problems were confronting. We went from dealing with one parent home issues, to teen parenting issues, to drug problems, to gender identification.

How do we handle the big changes that come into the lives of teens involved in our ministries? These changes have the potential to tear your staff apart and end the ministry.

Let me give an example: In 2019 we are dealing with issues of gender identification, and we have staff who are all over the board in regards to it. We were planning a retreat but we couldn't figure out how to deal with some of the students who self-identified as the opposite sex. Do we have a separate room at the hotel on the retreat? If so, what staff do we put in there? It was a very tough discussion and we weren't sure what to do.

After the meeting Carole and I talked about it, prayed about it and thought about it. Then one of our wise volunteers messaged me and asked a question which led me to an answer. "Why does this ministry exist?"

We exist to introduce teenagers to Jesus. We don't exist to showcase or crusade for social issues. We went back to the staff with that thought. Whatever events we did with the teens needed to fulfill our mission which is to reach out to teens, connect with them in positive relationships, introduce them to Jesus, help them grow in their faith, and discover God's purpose for their lives. Many of the volunteers who helped us develop that purpose statement are still with us in ministry.

For the time being we decided to hold off on the retreat because the focus would be on that specific social issue. All else would take a back seat. Social issues do need to be discussed at times, but the main focus of this event needed to be about them and Jesus.

When in doubt as to what you should or shouldn't do as far as events in your youth ministry, go back to your purpose statement. Regardless of the issues of the day, remember why you exist as a youth ministry. That will help you stay on track.

Carole's Note

Whatever the issue, God's command is to love Him and love others. Check your own heart and belief system when these issues arise. Are you basing your reactions to them on biblical truth, or on your upbringing? Are you uncomfortable because the Holy Spirit is telling you something is wrong, or because this is a new phase in the world? Change is hard. Staying strong biblically is harder. Don't give in to social pressure if it is against the word. And always show love to the teens who are dealing with the tough social issue of their time

Chapter 58

Changes

You've probably seen the person that refuses to get older. They're like the bald guy doing the comb over. You want to yell "Hey dude, you're not fooling anyone but yourself! You're bald!" The same goes with the person trying not to look old. They get plastic surgery, drive fast cars, wear clothes that young people wear, and carry on a lifestyle inappropriate for them

I look at those people and think, "Just grow old gracefully". Sometimes that's not as easy as it might seem. My grandfather used to say that growing old is not for the weak. As I age, the younger staff and students will see me carrying something and run over to me and want to help me with it. Meanwhile, I'm thinking. "WHAT!? That only happens to old people." Well, I've got news for myself. I'm getting older, losing energy, and having guilt feelings for not being able to keep up. Those thoughts led me to consider our ministry over the decades, where we are now, and how I should feel about it.

I started working in youth ministry with middle schoolers as a college intern. As I am writing this, I am in my sixty's with grown children and seven grandchildren. Sometimes I get a little depressed that I don't have the energy I once had in ministry. Our work with youth has taken many turns and changes. I don't always like it, but it's inevitable as we grow older and our life situation evolves. We've had to stop doing certain things, and other parts of the ministry have been handed over to younger staff. Sometimes as society evolves, that will change ministry as well. For example: we used to put on a big "Battle of the Bands" event every year because there were many teen bands around. It was a huge event and drew in many new teens to the ministry every year. Now there are very few teen bands so the event is no longer relevant.

We used to take a spring break trip down south. But as we've gotten older and the trip became too hard on us we've had to stop that event because there was no one else who was able to take it over. It also became too costly, and even too dangerous with the changes in society.

Ministry for me and for Carole has evolved. Once I had only myself to consider. I had tons of energy when I was a twenty year old college intern working with middle school students.

Then I got married. Eight years later we adopted our first daughter. Over the next ten years we adopted our other two daughters. Our children went through school, each one very different from the other, and were involved in very different activities. We then went through watching our children grow up and move out. Marriage, grandchildren, and empty nest.

As we have experienced all of those phases in life, our ministry has changed as a result. I've noticed it more lately as I've been self-evaluating, comparing my first days in ministry with today, and I've realized how different it is now than when I first started. Some of the changes I like, some of them I don't. I go through feelings of guilt for not being as active as I think I should be. I fight feelings of inadequacy, not having the energy that I used to have, or even the desire to do things the way I used to.

But I've come to the conclusion that I need to be okay with ministry being different now. And yes, I can even enjoy the different phases of ministry. Our roles will continue to change, as Carole and I are in the process of grooming our replacements. We gave birth to this outreach ministry. It's our life's work and we will continue to support it and stay involved in new ways as we move into the next phase of our own lives. And we'll enjoy that change as much as we can. We have accepted and enjoyed each phase of ministry as life moved forward. I think that's part of being able to have longevity in ministry.

Carole's Note

We have "fought the good fight...finished the race...kept the faith" (2 Timothy 4:7 NIV). We want to end well. We want to stay where God wants us and get out of the way when we need to. We have lived this ministry. We have a passion to see teens come to Jesus, and we will do all we can to see that happen, for as long as we can.

We feel God's hand of blessing on us as we begin our long good bye. We are youth ministers. We are also husband and wife. We are human bodies in need of rest. We are parents and grandparents. God knows if and when we will exit this ministry life. And we will be thankful that God allows times of retirement to enjoy each other, our family, and other aspects of life beyond ministry. We pray that God will make us willing to do what He wants in His time.

Enjoy every aspect of ministry. Don't neglect the life around you. Fight the good fight!

Afterward

This book was written from the perspective of working with unchurched teenagers, which we've done most of our ministry years. When we first began working with youth there was much more of a divide between families of church kids and unchurched. As American society has evolved the gap has narrowed.

Now days, my youth pastor friends are dealing with more unchurched youth than ever before. In fact, some of them work almost exclusively with un-churched students, either because their church teens won't attend youth group or because many of the church's families have similar values and attitudes as the unchurched families and students that they work with. So we believe that most of the material in our book will be relevant to any kind of youth work

When I was a young youth worker I thought I knew it all. I would attend youth conferences involving many different ministries and wonder who the old dudes were, and why they were still coming to a youth conference. Did they actually think they could still be effective with youth? As I got to know some of them and grew a few years older, I listened to some of their advice and stories, wishing I had paid more attention to the wisdom and knowledge they shared before I made some pretty big mistakes. I realized I would much rather learn from their mistakes than my own.

So I began to log some things that would have been valuable lessons for me as a younger youth guy. As the years passed, I was the one telling stories and giving advice. Now at sixty-three (at this writing) some of the local youth workers told me I should put my experiences and the lessons I'd learned out there for future youth workers to tap into.

Viola! This book. I hope it helps.

Printed in the United States
By Bookmasters